From coppersmith to nurse:
Alyosha
the son of a Gypsy chief

From coppersmith to nurse:
Alyosha
the son of a Gypsy chief

Gunilla Lundgren, Alyosha Taikon
Edited and translated by Donald Kenrick
Illustrated by Amanda Eriksson

CENTRE DE RECHERCHES TSIGANES
UNIVERSITY OF HERTFORDSHIRE PRESS

The *Interface Collection* is co-ordinated and developed by the
Gypsy Research Centre at the Université René Descartes in Paris.

The views expressed in this work are the authors and do not necessarily reflect those of the
publisher nor of the Gypsy Research Centre or its research groups
(historians, linguists, education specialists, etc.).

The Director of the *Interface Collection* is Jean-Pierre Liégeois

Published in Swedish by Bonnier Carlsen, 1999
And in Romani by Podium, 2002

This English edition published in Great Britain in 2003 by
University of Hertfordshire Press
Learning and Information Services
University of Hertfordshire
College Lane
Hatfield,
Hertfordshire AL10 9AB

ISBN 1 902806 22 0 paper back

© Text: Gunilla Lundgren and Alyosha Nils-Erik Dimiter Taikon 1998
English translation by Donald Kenrick
Romani translation by Hasse J. Columbus and Jonny G. Ivanovitch
© Drawings: Amanda Eriksson 1998

The right of Gunilla Lundgren and Alyosha Nils-Erik Dimiter Taikon to be identified as
authors of this work have been asserted by them in accordance with the
Copyright, Designs and Patents Act 1988.

All rights reserved. No part of this book may be reproduced or utilised in any form or by any means,
electronic or mechanical, including photocopying, recording or by any information storage and
retrieval system, without permission in writing from the author.

British Library Cataloguing in Publication Data
A catalogue record for this book is available from the British Library.

Design by Geoff Green, Cambridge CB4 5RA.
Cover design by John Robertshaw, Harpenden AL5 2JB
Printed in Great Britain by Antony Rowe Ltd., Chippenham SN14 6LH

Frontispiece: the author, Alyosha Taikon

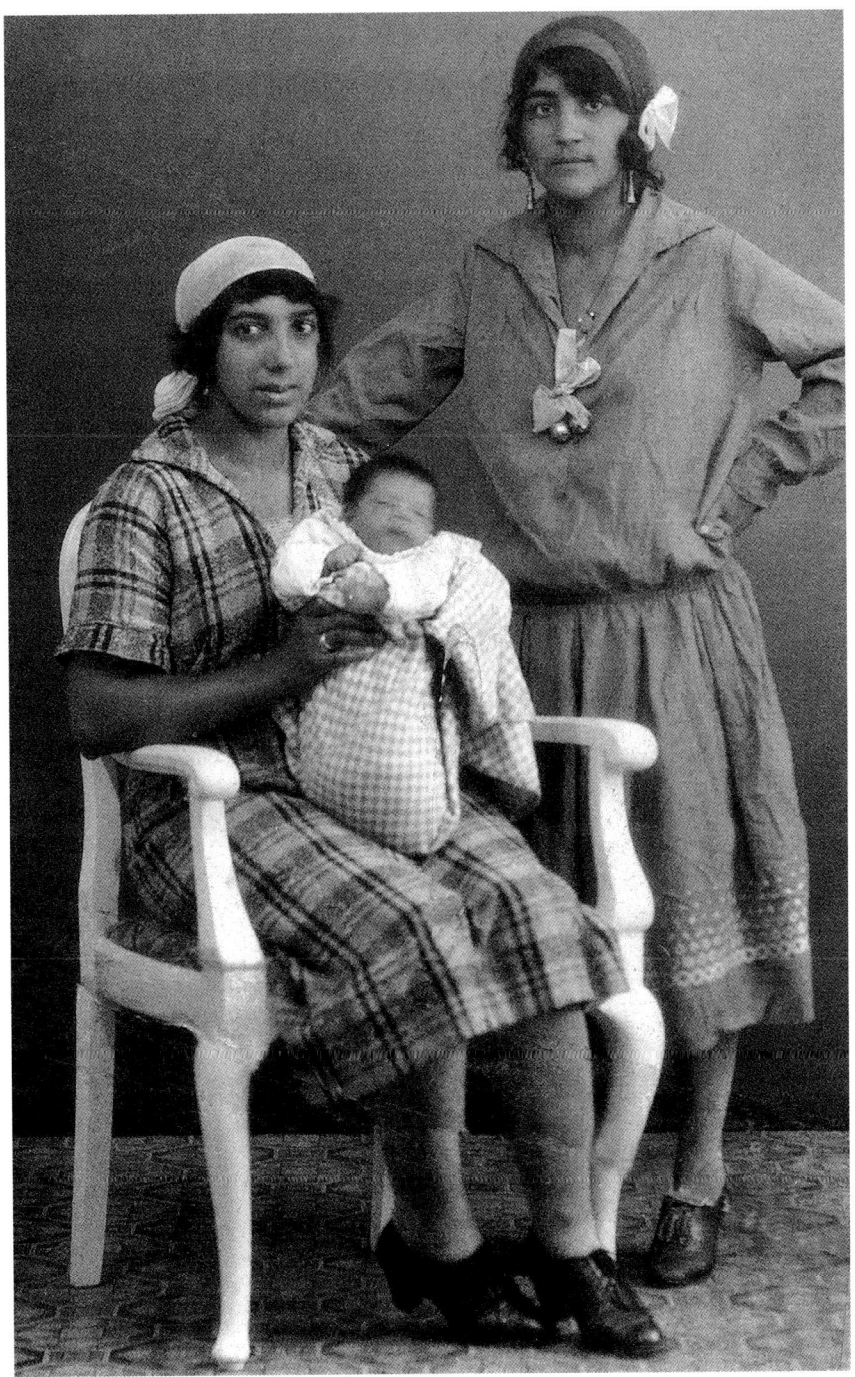

Me on Aunty Olga's knee. Next to us is my oldest brother's wife Roza

Me pe muřa bibiake la Olgake čanga. Paše muře praleski řomni e Roza

So si ande kniška

Introduction: Donald Kenrick　　　　　　　　　　xi

JEKHTO PARTJA
JEKM KAKAVIARI AUILO INFIRMER
ALJOŠA, O ŠIAV LE BIREVOSKU

Sas pe kai nas pe: Gunilla Lundgren		2
1	Kana arakhadjilem	6
2	Muřo dad	12
3	O papo ai e mami	16
4	O vurdon	20
5	Kakaviaria ai hanomos	26
6	O tivoli	32
7	Muři dei	42
8	O khelimos	46
9	Drabarimos	50
10	O duito marimos	58
11	Jekh nevo trajo ando Stockholmo	64
12	E bar ando Sköndal	74
13	Milai opre ando Švedo	78
14	Škola ande tsera	82
15	Jekh raieski avlin ando Tantolunden	90

Contents

Introduction: Donald Kenrick   xi

PART ONE
FROM COPPERSMITH TO NURSE:
ALYOSHA, THE SON OF A GYPSY CHIEF

Preface: Gunilla Lundgren		3
1	My birth	7
2	My Dad	13
3	Grandfather and grandmother	17
4	The caravan	21
5	Copper-smithing and tin-plating	27
6	The fairground	33
7	Mum	43
8	Dancing	47
9	Fortune-telling	51
10	The Second World war	59
11	A new life in Stockholm	65
12	The camp in Sköndal	75
13	Summers in the Northland	79
14	The tent school	83
15	A fine villa in Tantolunden	91

16	O vužimos	96
17	Gina	100
18	Abiav	104
19	Buči, kher ai glati	111

Romane paramičia   143

16	Cleanliness and purity	97
17	Gina	101
18	Marriage	105
19	Work, a flat – and children	111

PART TWO JOHAN TAIKON'S TALES

Introduction 124

1	The magic goldfish	125
2	The Gypsy who made his confession	129
3	The cut corn that raised itself	131
4	The big snake	133
5	The cunning boy and the beautiful Gypsy girl	138

Glossary to the Romani 143

Patretsi/Photographs
Fotografiska museet (Anna Riwkin) pp. 93, 95, 113
IMS Bildbyrå o angluno patreto ai/frontispiece p. 87 (A. Rygin)
pp. 28, 37, 67, 76, 84, 85, 106, 107
Malcolm Jacobson p. ii
Nordiska museets bildbyrå pp. 4, 9, 15, 19, 20, 25,
29, 45, 61, 68, 71, 81, 91, 97
Pressens Bild p 49
Sveriges Television AB Bildarkivet p. 35

Le kaver patretsi si katar o Aljoša Dimitri Taikon
či žjanglolpe kon la le patretsi
The other photos are from the collection of Alyosha Dimitri Taikon,
unknown photographers

Introduction

Part One of this book is the life story of Alyosha as told to Gunilla Lundgren and sympathetically edited by her for publication in Swedish and in a later Romani edition translated from the Swedish. Part Two contains some typical stories told by Alyosha's father, Johan, in Romani and recorded on audio tape in 1949.

The University of Hertfordshire Press decided to publish Part One in English and Romani on facing pages so that it could also be used as an aid for non-Gypsies who are learning the language and by the many Romanies who increasingly wish to read books in their own tongue. The Kalderash dialect was chosen for the translation because it was Alyosha's own dialect. It is also widely understood by many Swedish Roma who speak other varieties of Romani, not to mention large communities of so-called Vlah Gypsies throughout the world (also spelt Vlach or Vlax). They emigrated from Wallachia in Romania, their homeland, before emancipation from slavery and their dialect is very similar to Kalderash. It is, in fact, the most widely spoken Romani dialect and an obvious choice for persons wishing to learn Romani. Part Two was recorded in Kalderash but for copyright reasons is only published in English. Further guidance on learning Romani is given towards the end of this introduction

The Taikon family has held a leading position in Swedish Romany life since arriving there from Russia in the nineteenth century. Alyosha broke away from tradition by marrying a non-Gypsy (the second person in his family to do so) but more so by becoming a nurse, an occupation seen as *mahrime* (unclean) by the Romanies. Gunilla Lundgren explains in the preface to Part One how he came to recount in Swedish his story which was first published in Sweden in 1998 and then in a translation into the Kalderash dialect of Romani two years later.

Some history

The following introduction will be of help to English readers who are unfamiliar with the early history and way of life of Swedish Gypsies.

The Romany Gypsies left India more than a thousand years ago, possibly in search of work or because continual fighting made it impossible for them to travel from village to village practising their crafts and by 1500 they had reached most parts of Europe. The first Gypsies in Sweden came from Denmark in 1512 despite the two countries being at war as Swedish nationalists fought to free their homeland from Danish control. The town register of Stockholm for that year describes the visit of dark-skinned nomads. There were more immigrants later, this time from the east, from Estonia.

In 1523 when Gustav Vasa became king of an independent Sweden, he wrote an open letter to the Gypsies, telling them to leave the country, and a number of Gypsies did indeed leave and migrated to Finland. In 1560 the protestant Archbishop Petri told the priests not to baptise or bury Gypsies but his order was repealed in 1586 when priests were told they should try and baptise children, teach parents the Christian faith and encourage them to settle down. Eight years later a meeting of church leaders at Linköping reversed this decision, and the previous policy was re-adopted.

In 1637 a new law was passed stating all Gypsies must leave the country or the men would be executed and the women forcibly expelled. This was the first time the word *Zigenare* was used for Gypsies in Swedish. Previously, they had been called *Tattare,* being confused with the Turkish Tartars. Nowadays, official sources are more frequently using the word *Rom* – their own word for themselves in the Romani language. You will sometimes see this word spelt *Rrom*, as the initial 'r' in this word is pronounced differently from the 'r' in most European languages.

Despite these laws there are no cases are known of Gypsies being executed in Sweden. Finally, in 1748 a new decree was published banishing Gypsies who had not been born in Sweden. It is thought that a substantial number of Romanies stayed in the country in defiance of the law and merged with Swedish nomads, forming a minority group which is still sometimes called by the pejorative name *Tattare* but now more generally known as *Resande* (Travellers).

In 1860 entry restrictions were lifted, resulting in a new wave of immigration, principally of Alyosha's clan. These Kalderash Gypsies had left Romania and travelled in Russia after their liberation from a form of serfdom that was not very different from the slavery in the United States. Many Kalderash, however, were classed as slaves of the Princes of Wallachia and Moldova and were permitted to travel in the course of their work, providing they paid taxes to their Prince. These former slaves were the first to leave when the yoke was lifted from their shoulders. The Swedish census of 1922 recorded 250 Romany Gypsies and 1,500 *Tattare* (*Resande* or Travellers) but the Romani Gypsies had increased to 453 by the time of a further census in the middle of the Second World War. Sweden was one of the few countries not occupied by Nazi Germany and its Gypsies were spared from persecution. Indeed, it is now known that a small number of Romanies from Denmark were smuggled into the country alongside escaping Jews. Elsewhere in Europe the genocide had between a quarter and half a million Gypsy victims.

The Swedish government repealed earlier legislation in 1954 and limited immigration began. In 1960 the state took responsibility for housing Gypsies, and nomadism for practical purposes ended apart from those families who had travelling fairs, as did the family of Alyosha. At the time, there were about 100 sedentary and 125 nomadic families but within five years fewer than ten families remained in caravans.

In 1963 Katrina Taikon, the author's cousin, published her first book, *Zigenerska*, which called on the government to recognise the rights of her people. She later wrote a series of semi-autobiographical stories for children based on a fictitious Romany girl called Katitzi.

As a result of her campaign the government decided to set up a policy of 'organised importation' of Gypsies – a form of quota. In recent years considerable numbers of Gypsies have arrived from Eastern Europe and Yugoslavia, outnumbering the descendants of those Romanies who arrived at the end of the nineteenth century. Since the political changes in the east fewer immigrants are being accepted from those countries. Many hundreds of Finnish Gypsies have also immigrated to Sweden. Some 2,500 descendants of the earlier Kalderash immigrants now live in Sweden among a total estimated Gypsy population of 20,000. Apart from Katerina, another of Alyosha's cousins, Rosa, makes high-class jewellery while Hans Calderas is a popular singer. The education authorities have introduced mother-tongue teaching in Romani and special classes for adults to improve their education. Many Gypsies now take part in these programmes as teachers or assistants. A number of books have been published in Romani, both original (such as *O Tari ai e Zerfi* – a romantic ballad) and translations of Swedish children's books.

Both the Gypsies and the Travellers have set up self-help organisations while Finnish Gypsies in Sweden are represented by their own association. Although the Gypsies were presumably Hindus when they left India, they adopted the religion of the countries where they later lived. So we find in Sweden Catholics and Orthodox Christians as well as Muslims, while the Gypsy Pentecostal church is also active. Many Scandinavian Gypsies are active in the International Romani Union and a newly-formed organisation for writers, the International Romani Writers' Association. The Romany flag can be seen at meetings – blue and green with a red wheel. The blue is the sky and green represents meadows and fields. As the notes to the original Swedish edition say, the red wheel symbolises freedom and progress

The Romani language

Romani is a language related to Hindi and Punjabi but has split into several dialects. Kalderash is the most widely spoken and several grammars and dictionaries have been published. There are well over a million speakers and they can be found in almost every country in the world and for this reason alone it is a good dialect for beginners to learn. The author, Matéo Maximoff, a distant relative of Alyosha, translated the Bible into Romani but so far only the New Testament and Psalms have been published.

A good introduction to Romani – which does not, however, teach the language – is *What is the Romani Language?* also published by the University of Hertfordshire Press. Dr Ian Hancock, by birth part English Gypsy and part Vlah Romani and by profession a linguist at the University of Texas, has written a grammar describing Kalderash and other dialects which stem from Wallachia and adjacent territories, hence the title *A Handbook of Vlax Romani* (Slavica, 1995*)* and an extensive appendix on the language is included in his most recent book, *We are the Romani People* (University of Hertfordshire Press, 2002).

Dictionaries include Georges Calvet's *Dictionnaire Tsigane-Français* (L'Asiathèque,1993). The Chandigarh journal *Roma* published a series of lessons from 1974 while the French Bible Society published the New Testament and Psalms translations by the French writer Matéo Maximoff. Sweden, as stated above, has also seen a number of publications in Romani, primarily children's books.

DONALD KENRICK

Useful addresses for books in and about Romani:

Cottage Books, Rempstone Road, Gelsmoor, Coleorton, LE67 8HR

Etudes Tsiganes, 59 rue de l'Ourcq, Paris 75018, France

Romanestan Publications, 22 Northend, Warley, Essex CM14 5LA

See also the websites listed in *What is the Romani Language*?

PART ONE

From coppersmith to nurse:
Alyosha
the son of a Gypsy Chief

Sas pe kai nas pe…

But berš garada o Nils-Erik Dimiter jekh sekreto. Šoha či phenelas pesko čačo anav o řomano ai kana pušenas les sostar sas kadia kalo, vo phenelas ke ande les anda Řusia sar glata (baistruko) ai barilo ando Dalarna (jekh rig ando Švedo).
Numa vo si řom.
Akana lape te phenel mange o Aljoša Nils-Erik Dimiter Taikon pesko trajo mange.
Jekh data o kurko ande jekhe beršeski vriama, maladjuvavas lesa pala leski šukar skafidi. O Aljoša da man te xav gulasch, sarmi ai tsoda mange whiskey. Vo mutsolas ai me ramovas. But asaiam ande jekh tsan numa butivar trobulas o Aljoša vi te anel pesko baro parno nosoviko de but kai rovelas.
Lesko trajo si jekh interesanto historia ande le berš 1900.
Numa kana tsodam ame te rodas te arakhas patreturia kai malaven pala leski historia (divano) atunči nas ame but hazna anda kudola patretsi kai sas les khere. Nas les či patretsi de glata, či patretsi školake varke abiaveske.
– Kai sas ame mašinki patretonge ande le tseri! phenelas o Aljoša.

Le patretsi kai si ande kadia kniška musai sas te rodas le ande le museeuria ai kai le gazetaria. But anda le patretsi kai či arakhasas musai sas te ramo le e Amanda Eriksson anda vas, te šai maladjol pala e historia le Aljošaski.
Tumna ande vurma la kniškaki sikavel tuke anda le paramičia kai phenelas lesko dad paša jag.

GUNILLA LUNDGREN

Preface

It was like this and then it wasn't like this.

For many years Nils-Erik Dimiter kept a secret. He never used his full name and if anyone asked why he was so dark he said he was an adopted Russian child from Dalarna.

He is a Gypsy.

Now Alyosha has told me the story of his life.

Once a week for a whole year we met at his finely laid kitchen table. Alyosha invited me to goulasch, stuffed cabbage and whiskey. He spoke and I wrote. We laughed a lot but sometimes Alyosha needed to get out his large white handkerchief and cry.

His life is a gripping story from the twentieth century.

When we needed to find interesting pictures that would go with his story we didn't get much help from Alyosha's photo album.

There were no pictures of childhood, school reports or wedding photos.

"We didn't have any cameras in our tents," explained Alyosha.

Looking for the book's photos led us to museum archives and newspaper records. What we couldn't find in the archives Amanda Eriksson drew from Alyosha's descriptions. At the end of the book there are some pages with stories which Alyosha's father used to tell at the fireside.

"It was like this and yet it wasn't like this,
but if it hadn't happened it wouldn't have been told."

Alyosha's father, Johan Dimitri Taikon, always began like this when he told stories by the camp fire. I think that makes a good introduction to this book.

GUNILLA LUNDGREN

These are relations of Alyosha's mother who travelled in Denmark. King Frederik VIII said they could remain in the country. And they called them the King's Gypsies. But when the King died they pushed them all out of Denmark into Sweden. They only let one girl remain. The photograph is from 1900.

Kadala si niamuri le Aljošaske deiasa kai phirenas ando Denemarko. Lenge phenda o amperato o Frederik VIII anda Denemarko ke šai bešen ando tsem. Ta lenge phenenas le amperatoske řom. Kana o amperato mulo šiude savoren avri anda Denemarko ando Švedo. Ferdi jekha šeia mukle te bešel. Patreto anda berš 1900.

Alyosha's father and mother with their oldest grandchild Erland in Gävle. 1934

Le Aljosaško dad ai leski dei ai o mai phuro neputo o Erland ando Gävle. 1934.

JEKHTO ŠERO

Kana arakhadjilem

Te phenel o manuš pa pesko trajo nai vušoro. Si but djeli kai či kamel o manuš te serel, si djeli ai buča kai či kamel o manuš te žjanel, ai si djeli kai či kamel o manuš dareš te phenel.

Žjanav kai arakhadjilem, numa či žjanav o berš. Le berš kai si ramome ando muřo lil numa tsodine le te bušolpe. Kudo so žjanav pa muře berš de glata, žjanav ke phenda mange jekh anda muře kak.

Sas pe jekh riat ando maškar le milasko ando Norrlando (dur opre ando Švedo) mai but sar 70 berš palpale. Muři dei e Volja bešelas ande kasa ande amaro tivoli (feria). Kotse angla laki tsera kerdjila jekh bari kola, katar le but gažje kai avile te dikhen so keren le řom. Maškar le but selči pala e tsera phabonas le but lempi, but fialuria ferbi, ai ašundjolas e djili katar e draška, (garmunia) ai vi ašundjolas but mui ai bašimos katar le raketi (petarduri) katar le grastoře (karuseli) ai kai del o manuš puške. Siguro sas te keren laše love kudia šukar riat, le činčaria sovenas ai le norrlandaria kamenas ferdi te khelen.

Pe jekh data uštili muři dei opre ai lape te čipil ta le gažje parnile ando mui. Khonik ande kola či aliarenas laki šib. Numa la bibia Olgako řom strazom mukla e karusela ai našlo avri po drom ži ando gavořo kai bušolas Nordmaling. Kotse arakhla jekh doxtoritsa glatengi, voi avili ži kai amari vatra.

Dui vai trin časuria pala kudo arakhadjilem me o Aljoša Nils-Erik Dimiter Taikon, jekh tati riat ande jekh tsera pe jekh kimpo (tsan) kai khelel peske o manuš pe menča ando Ångermanland.

Činořo ai kovlo simas. Muři dei tsoda inja glaten pe lumia mai anglal mandar, dui anda lende xasarda (mule) mai čiřa vi man sas te xasarel. Tena avilo pala jekh phuri kai sas amende ande bar, savoře phenenas ke

CHAPTER ONE

My birth

It's not easy to tell one's life story. One doesn't want to remember everything, there are things one doesn't know and other things one doesn't want to recount. I know where I was born but not the year. The dates in my passport are just made up numbers. What I know about my birth is what one of my uncles told me.

It was a midsummer's evening in the Northland more than seventy years ago. My mother, Volja, looked after the till for our circus. In front of her tent stood a queue of inquisitive Swedes. Lamps shone among the booths and kiosks behind the tent and accordion music mingled with shouts and shots from the roundabout and shooting booths. A fine evening like this would bring in good money and while the midges slept, the locals would want to dance the fox-trot.

Suddenly mother stood up and screamed so loudly that the Swedes went white. No one in the queue could understand what she was shouting. But Aunt Olga's husband left his booth straightaway and ran along the main road right up to Nordmaling. There he found a midwife who came back to the camp with him.

I was born a few hours later, Alyosha Nils-Erik Dimiter Taikon, under the midnight sun in a tent on a football field in Angermannland.

I was small and weak. Mother had given birth to nine children before me, she had lost two and I might also have passed away. But there was an old woman in the camp whom people said was a witch. She was to be my godmother.

drabarni la. Voi aresli te avel muři čirvi.

– Anen orde le šavořes! phenda e phuri. Činav les me pe jekh biaria.

Pala kudo la ai bilada molivi ai mukelas te pečal o molivi ande jekh čaro pajesa opral pa muřo šero. Kadia kerda voi te traiv.

Dui, trin kurke pala kudia vuže sas man vi dui čirve, von sas švedaia gažje, jekh sas o masari ai o kaver sas kai bičinelas zelenimata ando gavořo. Kotse ando gav vi bolde ma ande khangeri ai dine ma o anav Aljoša, pala o šiav le amperatosko ande Řusia, ai vi Nils-Erik gažjikano anav.

Muře dades ai muřa da sas la vuže šiov šiave: Fardi, Muto, Vošo, Wilhem, Josef ai o Folke.

So fugo sičile te phiren gata lenaspe sa pala amaro dad, sičile te hanon, te lašiaren maturi ai piria, dareš vi le karuseli ai e feria lašiarenas. Lenge vas sa šuvle ai melale sas.

Me mai fugo lavas ma pala muři dei, ke muře vas sas činoře ai kovle. Me naštivas te dikhav melale piria vai řuzinime maturi. Prasanas man la dako šiav. Me gindiv ke muřa dake mišto sas ke lavas man sa pala late, ke mai anglal sar te arakhadjovav me, voi kamelas jekh šei te šai žutil la kai vasuria. Numa akana mai bine sas la jekh šiav kai sičolas te tsol čajo ai te khosel peske dadeske čalia.

My birth

My older brothers, Fardi, Muto and Vosho about 1915. Muto died of food poisoning a few years later.

Muře pral le phure Fardi, Muto ai Vošo. O Muto mulo oni berš pala kudo.

"Give the boy here", said the old lady. "I'll buy him for a beer".

Then she melted some lead and poured it drop by drop into a bowl of water held over my head. So she arranged that I should live.

A few weeks later I got two godfathers, they were Swedes. They were a butcher and a grocer from Nordmaling. I was baptised in the church there and was called Alyosha after the Russian Csar's son. Nils-Erik was my Swedish name.

Mother and father already had six sons: Fardi, Muto, Vosho, Wilhem, Josef and Folke.

As soon as they could walk they followed their father about, learning how to re-tin, and repair kitchen pots and pans and car bodies. They looked after the roundabouts and fairground booths. Their hands got rough and dirty.

I preferred to be with mother, my hands were small and soft. I hated dirty pots and rusty cars. People said I was a mummy's boy. Mother was

Činořo šavoro simas kana vuže vazdavas e pari planča ai tačaravas la po bov, te plančiv muře pralenge gada. Anavas pai, řandavas kolumpiria ai xalavavas le vasuria, šilavavas ande tseri ai ande vurdona. Te na gindin ke pe zor keravas buči, mange sas drago te avel vužo ai čistome.

Muřa deia ai dades manas le kaver glati pala mande, numa sa kadia mai barili e familia. Kana muřo kak o Vošo ai leski řomni e Lutka mule ando jekh nasfalimos kai bušolas kolera (pono) atunči ašile lenge glati korkořo ai pusto. Dui anda le glati ašile amende, me či djinavas le sar veri numa sar muře pral, ai akana vuže samas oxto žjene ande familia.

Ame samas opral pa 40 žjene kai phirasas ande jekh tsan. Muřo papo sas o mai phuro ai me simas o mai terno. Ame phirasas pe antrego Švedo, katar jekh foro kai bušolas Trelleborg kai si tele ando Švedo ži ando Kiruna kai si tumna dur opre ando Švedo, amentsa phiravasas amari tivoli, amare tseri, vurdona, maturi, traktoruri ai rimorki. Ferdi o papo inke tradelas sar kerenas mai anglal, grastesa ai vurdonesa.

Kana sas e doba le ivendeski rodasas jekh tsan kai šai bešas mai lungo vriama ai te anzaras amare tseri, te na phiras but po baro šil. So avelas o milai pale peravasas ai tradasas. Antrego berš ando milai phirasas katar godi ai bešasas o mai but dui kurke pe svako tsan.

Muřo dad vai muře pral žjanastar butivar mai anglal te rodel tsana kai si laše, ai te mangen slobodia katar le gažje kai porončin pe tsana ai le kimpuria. Te si ke kamasas te bešas pe jekh kimpo trobulas te pušas katar o mužiko te šai mukel amen po tsan, var te sas tsan kai porončilas o kher le forosko trobulas te pušas katar o baro kotsar.

But djeli trobulas lašiarde mai anglal: naprimer katar te len o pai? Trobulas te len mišto sama te na phabaren le gažjengi čar, kai šai xan djiv le paposke gras, sodi muken te bešas? Sodi love mangen? Kudolendar djesa sas kai khosavas muře dadeske čalia mai mišto, ai khosavas leske papuči ta strefianas ai vi leski peleria borsalino anda barxato strefialas šukar.

quite happy about this. She had wanted a daughter when I was born, a girl who could help her with the housework. Now she had a boy who had to learn to make tea and clean father's dark suits.

I was only a little tiddler but I could already heat up the heavy iron and iron my brothers' shirts. I fetched water, peeled potatoes and washed up, I swept inside the tent and wagons. There was nothing I didn't like, I liked everything that was polished and clean.

Mother and father didn't have any more children after me but the family grew anyway. When Uncle Vosho and his wife Lutka died of cholera in Gävle their children became orphans. We took two of them in and they became my brother and sister. I didn't think of them as being cousins any more. Now there were eight children in the family.

There were well over forty of us who travelled together. Grandpa was the oldest and I was the youngest. We travelled over the whole of Sweden, from Trelleborg in the south to Kiruna in the far north, we had our circus with us with all the tents and wagons, cars, tractors and stands. Only grandpa travelled in the old way with a horse and cart.

In the winter we tried to find a camping place where we could put up our tents and stay there during the coldest weather. When it got warmer in the spring we broke camp. All the rest of the year we travelled around and stayed fourteen days at the most in any one place.

Father, or some of my brothers, would travel, ahead and look for a place we could move to. They had to see that the site was good enough and talk to the owner of the field. If we were going to set up camp on a farmer's field he had to be talked to; if it was the council's land, then they had to find the estate manager.

There was a lot to discuss: where could we get water, what about the danger of fires, where could grandpa's horses graze, how long could we stay, what would it cost?

It was for these trips that I had to brush father's dark suit, his shoes and shiny hat.

DUITO ŠERO

Muřo dad

Muřo dad bušolas Miloš. Gažjikanes phenelas peske Johan Dimitri Taikon. Vo arakhadjilo ando Ungriko numa areslo ande Řusia kana sas činořo. Vo delas duma pe efta šiba: řomanes, řusiska, polčiska, lettiska, niamtsiska, finlandesiska, ai švediska. Bisterdem ke vi denamarkiska ai norvegiska žjanelas; kudia si inja šiba. Vo phirelas pe antrego Europa peska familiasa, foro forostar, tsem tsemestar. Pala o marimos ando 1918, vo phirelas numa ando Švedo.

Muřo dad sas prinžardo sar jekh čačo ai godjaver manuš. Vo sas djindo vi maškar le gažje ai vi maškar le řom. Le gažjenge butivar presentilaspe sar o řomano birevo Taikon. Vo sas o šero la familiako.

Muřo dad žjanelas but paramiča. Sa kadia but paramiča žjanelas sar sodi ratja si ando berš. Ratjako kana phandavasas o tivoli ai le gažje žjanastar khere, atunči našasas ame le glati ando veš te anas kaš te šai keren jag. Onivar miazolas ke bi la jagako či žjan le paramiča.

Muřo dad phenelas le paramiča sar te avilosas kotse, ai kerelas anda le vas. Ame le glati gindisas ke so godi phenel sa čačimos, gindisas ke o gažjo kai arakhadjilo katar jekh grasni ke čačes si, ai ke amaro dad si kai atsada le rašas.

— Sas pe kai nas pe, te či avelas pe, či phenelas pe.

CHAPTER TWO

Dad

Dad was called Milosh. His official Swedish name was Johan Dimitri Taikon. He was born in Hungary and came to Russia when he was very small. He spoke seven languages: our own language – Romani – of course, Russian, Polish, Latvian, German, Finnish and Swedish. He also knew Danish and Norwegian so that made nine. He had travelled with his family back and forth through many European countries. After 1918 when the First World War was over he came to Sweden.

My father was known as an honest and clever man. He was respected by both Gypsies and Swedes. In front of Swedes he often introduced himself as Taikon, the Gypsy chief. He was our family's headman. Daddy was a great storyteller. He certainly knew as many stories as a year has nights. In the evenings when the fair was closed and the Swedes had gone back to their homes, we young ones would run amongst the trees and collect wood and twigs for a fire. It was as if there had to be a fire if the stories were to emerge.

Daddy told stories in a lively manner with gestures. We young ones believed that everything had actually happened, that he himself had met the man who was the child of a horse and that it was our own dad that had cheated the priest of the money.

"It was like this and yet it wasn't like this but if it hadn't happened I wouldn't be telling it."

Kadia lenaspe sa muře dadeske paramiča.

Muřo kak o Damo kana phenelas divanuria sas kaver fialo. Les sas les paramiča řusiska ande jekh kniška av vi djinelas anda e biblia. Me meravas anda leske histori, mai drago sas mange inke sar muře dadeske. Ande kudola kniški sas but zadački ai vorbi godjaver.

– Sostar si mišto te avel tu love? pušelas o kak o Damo.

– Šai čines tuke jekh gras, phendem me.

Kudo nas vurta atveto.

– Šai čines tuke jekh kuštik ruponi!

Pale bi-malado atveto.

O čačo atveto sas kadia: mišto si te avel tu love te na gindin varekon ke san čořo.

Muřo dad či žjanelas te djinel, vo garavelas sa peske paramiča ando šero. Kotse ando šero miazolas ke amboldel le patria sar ande jekh kniška ai ferdi ankalavelas ai ankalavelas, vi kutkar ai vi kutkar. Khonik či žjanelas kadia but pa amari vitsa, katar avenas kai žjanas sar muřo dad. Anda kudo kana godi les akharenas o pervo kana sas ka jekh kris řomani kai trobulas te pečil le řomen.

Savore pačanas lesko mui, ferdi jekh či pačalas lesko mui. O papo!

So began all his stories.

My Uncle Damo's stories were different. He had books of Russian tales and a bible that he would read from. I liked his stories even more than Dad's. They were full of riddles and proverbs.

"Why is it a good thing to have money?" asked Uncle Damo.

"You can buy a horse," I guessed.

That was wrong.

"You can get a silver belt made."

Wrong again.

The right answer to the riddle was – it is good to have money otherwise people think you are poor.

Dad could not read, he had all his stories in his head. He leafed through them there in his mind like a book, to and fro in time. No one knew more about our family and the travels of our people than Dad. That was why he was called in to judge when Gypsies quarrelled and wanted a court hearing.

Everyone obeyed Dad except for one person. His father.

Here you can see my family on tour with a performance of song and dance in Finland about 1914. Dad is standing the furthest to the right and Mum is the fourth person from the right, Next to her to the left is my oldest brother Fardi.

Katka muři familia keren jekh xoro djilango ai khelimasko ando Finland karing o berš 1914. Muřo dad si tumma pe čači rig ai muři dei si e štarto žuvli pa čačo vas. Pe laki stingo rig si muřo phuro pral o Fardi.

TRINTO ŠERO

O papo ai e mami

Muřo papo sas vuriado ande kale tsalia bare rupone kočakentsa. Vi vo phiravelas peleria borsalino anda barxato ai leske kheria sas bare ai kana godi strefianas zorales.

Onivar lelas muřo papo angle peski birevoska rovli kai sas la bija ruponi, ai tsolas anda koř pesko lantso kai kintirilas dui kili ai dopaš. Ande tsera bešelas numa nas čořo! Les sas les love řusiska (rubli) ai galbi kai phandelas po šelo ande jekh baro bufari.

Ande leski tsera sas les vi jekh jaštiko řusiska kotse garavelas vo peske sunakone angrustia, e kuštik ai pesko lantso ai vi le purane taxta le rupone. Kai kudo jaštiko sas jekh leketo rupono ai e čaia garavelas la ande posoči le laiberoski.

Le paposko jaštiko řusiako sas amaro banko. Kana sas vremi čoře atunči žjalas o papo kai kasa ai tsolas jekh taxtai rupono sar sumadji ai denas les love vunžile. Atunči trobulas te kerel love sar mai fugo te na xasavol e sumadji ai te bičindjol mai dur.

Oj Devla, če but šukar taxta, ai vešturi bičindjile ai bilade anda kudia ke nas love!

Muři mami arakhadjili ando Ungriko. La šoha či dikhlem

CHAPTER THREE

Grandfather and grandmother

Grandfather had a black suit with large shining silver buttons on it. Like my dad he had a velvet hat and his boots were high and well polished.

Sometimes grandfather took his chief's stick with a silver top and put on his chain of office which weighed 2.5 kilos. He lived in a tent but he certainly wasn't poor!

He had Russian banknotes and gold roubles in a thick wallet tied together with a string.

In his tent he had a trunk from Russia where he kept his golden rings, his belt, his chain and some old silver beakers. The trunk had a silver lock and grandfather kept the key in the pocket of his jacket.

Grandfather's Russian trunk was our bank. When hard times arrived grandfather went to the pawnshop and deposited a silver beaker. Then he could borrow money. Then we had to earn a few hundred crowns so we could redeem the beaker on time otherwise it would be sold on.

Oh, how many beautiful beakers and pieces of jewellery were lost and melted down because there was no money!

My grandmother was born in Hungary. I never met her. I am told she was quite hot-tempered. When one of her sons married a Swedish woman from Gothenburg, grandmother got so angry she took a log of firewood and banged herself on the head. She did it with such force that she had a cerebral haemorrhage and died.

Grandmother was a true fortune-teller, she could both see into the future and interpret the past. She could make deep wells run dry and runaway horses stop.

me. Numa phenen pa late ke jagali sas. Kana jekh anda lake šave ansurisailo jekha gažiasa atunči la voi ande bari xoli jekh kaš, ai dape kadia de zorales pa šero ta šurda la o rat ai muli.

E mami čači drabarni sas, voi šai dikhelas vi angle so sas te avel, ai vi so kerdjila de dumolt. Voi daštilas te kerel te šučon le xainga, ai le gras kai spurdjan te ašien.

Sas jekh data kana jekh žjuvli mužiškania kai či kamelas či jekh fialo te del pai muřa mamia anda peski xaing. Phenda ke či dela dareš sosi jekh řoi pai ka jekh řomni.

– Ašion tu gažio, čipisarda muři mami, tu gindis ke porončis po pai anda kudo ke e xaing čiri si! Numa o pai amaro Del da amen. Si te kijis tu!

Pe teharin kudia xaing šučili.

Grandfather and Grandmother

Grandmother with her grandson, Muto, around 1917. Grandfather had grandmother's silver belt made by a goldsmith by the name of Möller in Trondheim in Norway in 1916. At the same time my father ordered a similar belt for his young wife. In that belt there was a real diamond. That belt belongs to me now.

Muři mami peske neputosa le Mutosa karing berš 1917. Laki kuštik da o papo te kerel po zakazo ka jekh azintari kai bušolas Möller ando Trondheim Norvego ando berš 1916. Sa ande kudia vriama da vi muřo dad te keren pašti sar jekh fialo kuštik ka peski terni řomni. Numa ande kudia kuštik sa jekh diamanto tsodino. Ai kudia si muři adjes.

There once was a peasant woman who refused to give grandmother water from her well. Not even one cup to drink did she want to give to a Gypsy woman.

"You peasant woman", grandmother exclaimed, "you think you own this water because you own the well! But the water has been given to us from Our Lord. You'll regret this!"

On the next day the well ran dry.

ŠTARTO ŠERO

O vurdon

So godi trajilas e mami anelas vi voi love le drabarimasa, jekh žjuvli kai žjanelas te drabarel sas djindi ai respektime maškar amende le řom. So mai phuri sas kudia žjuvli mai djindi sas laki vorba. Numa kana godi le muršeski vorba sa mai bari sas ande vurma. Jekh phuro godjaver si djindo ai savoře ande familia musai te pačan lesko mui. O papo sas kasavestar manuš, ai khonik či žjanas lesa kontra.

Mai anglal sar te ansuril muřo dad muře phure prales, atunči tradales o papo te žjal ando Niamtso te činel jekh nevi karusela ka tivoli. Jekh nevi bori ande tsera si mai jekh mui te pravares, numa vi jekh ženo mai but kai buči te žutil.

The kitchen in the caravan

Kuxnia ando vurdon

CHAPTER FOUR

The caravan

For as long as she lived, grandmother helped to earn money by telling fortunes, and a woman who was good at telling fortunes became highly respected among us Gypsies. The older a woman got the more say she had. However, the man had the last word in the family. Everybody in the family had to obey a wise old man. Grandfather was such a man. Nobody went against what he said.

When Dad was to give my oldest brother away in marriage grandfather sent him to Germany to buy a new merry-go-round for the amusement park. A young daughter-in-law meant there would soon be more mouths to feed but also more family members who were able to work.

Muřo dad avilo anda Niamtso ai kerelas barimata. Vo phenda ke baro šefto kerda, vi phagla anda tsena, činda jekh karusela ai vi jekh vurdon pe le paposke love.

O papo mulo ande xoli! Šoha či mukela te avel jekh vurdon pe leski vatra!

O vurdon sas kerdo anda jekh svetlo kaš kai strefialas, oxto meteria de lungo ai vi veranda sas les. Paša e skara sas e kuxnia, ai porme avelas o salono, ai tumna ando fundo pala dui vudara kaštune sas e soba le suimaski. Kotse sas jekh baro pato kai la sa e soba.

O salono sas vuriado anda kovle lole barxatoske skamina ai ande škafuria sas šukar glindi tsodine andre. Ando čardako sas but činoře feliestri anda but ferbi. Kana marelas o kham pal feliestri kerdjolas but ferbi pe ziduria ai ande le glindi.

Numa le paposke nas bari djela. Šoha nas te pařovel peski tsera ai pesko gras pe jekh vurdon! Atunči manai o manuš libro ai puterdo. Vo či kamelas te aliarelpe tasado maškar le ziduria ai le glindi ande jekh vurdon, vo kamelas te tradel kana vo kamel, ai na te anklel po dježes. Ke jekh kasavestar baro vurdon naštinas te čirden le gras, musai sas po dježes te tson les.

Numa phenen so kamena numa o vurdon lašio šefto sas. Sar tsolas muři dei e plaka le drabarimaski po vurdon strazom šurdjonas le gažje pe late. Anda kudo ke le gažje merenas te dikhen sar miazol jekh řomano vurdon.

Sar me lovodivas kudo vurdon! O mai but kana sas ratja ivende ke čimai trobul te pavo ma ande tsera.

O vurdon sas amenge lašio vi kana sas te mučis ame pe kaver vetri (tsana) amen le glaten tsonas amen ando vurdon ai bešasas ande kudola lole barxatoske skamina ai o vurdon pe šinji le dježesoske. Dikhasas avri pa le feliestri, ai onivar kerasas anda le vas sar te avilamas amperaturia.

Kana aresasas kotse kai trobulas, atunči lenas le gažje tele o vurdon pa džežes, ai jekh traktoro čirdelas amen ži kai amari nevi vatra. Muře pral le mai phure ai le kaver žjene anda amari familia avenas ande amaro drom. Von aresenas jekh varke dui djes mai anglal le kaminontsa ai le traktorontsa.

Kon avelas ta pe vurma, o papo ke leske žjalas trin, štar vai panž djes žipo aresel amen. Lesko gras, e buči varke e vriama porončilas sodi žjal leske te avel.

The caravan

Dad returned from his trip and he was proud. He thought he had done a good piece of business, he had haggled over the price and managed to get both a merry-go-round and a barrel-organ as well as a caravan for grandfather's money.

Grandfather was furious! He never thought he would have to put up with a caravan in his Gypsy camp! The caravan was made of light brown varnished oak, eight meters long with a veranda. Next to the stairs was the kitchen, then there was the living room and in the back, behind two sliding doors of mahogany, was the bedroom. A large bed took up the whole room. The living room was equipped with soft, red velvet sofas and there were beautiful, cut mirrors on the doors of the wardrobes. In the ceiling there was a row of small windows made of coloured glass. When the sun was shining through, the colours made varied patterns on the walls and mirrors of the living room.

Grandfather wasn't impressed. He would never change his tent and his horse for a caravan! Then he would lose all his freedom. He didn't want to live shut up behind walls and mirrors. As the caravan was so large it couldn't be pulled by horses but had to be transported by train and grandfather wanted to set off when it suited him and not the train!

But the caravan turned out to be good for business. A queue formed immediately when my mother put up a sign saying she was telling fortunes in there. The Swedes were terribly curious and didn't know what they could do to get in and take a look inside a real Gypsy wagon. This was their chance.

How I sang the praises of this caravan! Especially in winter nights when I got out of being freezing cold in the tent.

The caravan was also good when we were moving for all of us kids were packed into it and we could sit on the red velvet sofas and go on the railway. We peeked through the windows of the caravan and sometimes we waved out in a stylish way, just as if we were royal highnesses.

At the end station of the journey the caravan was unloaded from the train and pulled by a tractor to our new camp site. My older brothers and most of the family welcomed us. They had arrived by car and tractors a few days earlier.

The very last one to arrive was grandfather, it could take him three, four or five days to catch up with us. The horse, work, the weather or something else which was unpredictable decided the speed of his trip.

O papo bešelas ande jekh tsera kai žjalas skutsome, panž koverči sas la ai dui poxtana tserake. Vo sovelas pe phuv bi khančesko numa vulojilaspe ande perina puxoski, ferdi kana sas šil vai čingo atunči tsolas soluma varke čače ponjevi telal.

Sogodi muři bibi e Olga nas ansurime tradelas vivoi le paposa. Voi drabarelas žipo o papo hanolas tigei, ai porme riatjako kana o papo anzarelas e tsera atunči voi tsolas pe te čiravel.

Ande lengo vurdonoře žjalas e tsera, le koverči, e perina, oni buže gadentsa, e tigaia kai sas le paposke klašturia ai djeli kai trobunas les kai buči, la Olgako jaštiko kai sas lake vasuria ai djeli kai trobul ande poriatka ai le paposko jaštiko kai sas leske vešturia sunakone ai rupone.

Žjanastar kana kamenas ai sas lentsa sas so trobul le.

Či porončilas khonik pe lende. Von sas libero.

Grandfather lived in a triangular tent made of five poles and two pieces of canvas. He slept on the bare ground with a feather eiderdown-wrapped around him. If the conditions were cold or wet he covered the ground with straw and hand-woven carpets.

For as long as his daughter, Aunt Olga, was unmarried she travelled together with grandfather. She told fortunes while grandfather did tinning and at night, when grandfather pitched the tent, she cooked for them.

On their cart there was room for the tent's canvas with the poles, the eiderdowns, some bundles of clothes, the cauldron with grandfather's working tools, Aunt Olga's trunk with kitchen utensils and grandfather's trunk with the gold and silver things.

They set off to travel when they wanted to and they kept everything they needed with them.

They were free.

The meals used to be cooked out in the open air. There was the cauldron on an iron tripod. In winter-time the fire was moved inside the tent. The photo is from Denmark at the end of the 1890s.

Mai anglal čiravenas o xabe avri pe kimpuri. E piri bešelas pe trin punře sastrune. Ivende mučinas e jag ande tsera., O paticto lo anda Denemarko de anda o berš 1890.

PANŽTO ŠERO

Kakaviaria ai hanomos

O papo žjanelas so si čino ai te na avel o manuš libro. Vo nakhlo o marimos kai mardape o Japono ai e Řusia ando 1905 ai vi o pervo marimos ando 1914–1918. Vo našlo anda Litva, Lettva, Estland ai o Finlando ži ando Švedo. Vo či kamelas te mudarel ai te marelpe ande či jekhe tsemeski ketenia, vo sas kakaviari ai na ketana!

Vo sas anda vitsa kalderaš, kudia vorba kamel te phenel le kakaviaria (bučarne kai keren buči xarkumasa). Lesko dad, ai papo ai vi o prapapo kerenas kadia buči ande xarkuma ai hanomos, sar kai kerelas muřo dad ai muře pral.

Sar aresasas pe jekh nevi vatra strazom žjanas muře pral kruglom ande khera kai sas paše, te mangen buča. Pušenas te sas le gažjen piria xarkune kai trobun hanome vai lašiarde? Atunči anenas pesa sa le xale ai rimome piria ande vatra. Pe teharin ingerenas palpale le gažjenge piria vurtome ai strefianas sar te avilosas neve anda e lavka. Či jekh semno ličarimos manas ai vi e zeleno kokliala lenas tele pe mašinka.

Le žjuvlian vai amen le glaten tradenas te ingeras palpale le piria kai sas lašiarde ai vužarde. Onivar denas amen love, onivar anře, jekh kajni, jekh gono kolompiria vai jekh phagi piri kai lašiarasas ai bičinasas ande kaver gav.

Pe kudia vriama pašti sa le piria sas kerde anda xarkuma.E xarkuma fugo rimolas pe ai zelenilas katar e kokliala, ai anklelas anda kudia sar vutrava vi le manušenge ai vi le žigenjenge. Anda kudo trobulas hanome e piri andral arčičesa. O arčiči trobulas tačardo te šai bilal ai te phirel mai vušoro.

CHAPTER FIVE

Copper-smithing and tin-plating

Grandfather knew what lack of freedom meant. He had survived the Russian-Japanese war in 1905 and the First World War in 1914–1918. He had fled through Lithuania, Latvia, Estonia and Finland to Sweden. He didn't want to kill or fight for the army of any country, he was a coppersmith and not a soldier!

He belonged to the Kalderash clan, this means the coppersmith Gypsies. His father, grandfather and great-grandfather, all worked with copper-smithery and tin-plating, just like my father and my brothers did now.

When we arrived at a new site my brothers went straight immediately to the houses near our camp and asked for work. Were there any copper pots which needed tin-plating or repairing? They took all the worn-out and broken items with them to the camp. The very next day the peasant or the lady of the house got back their possessions, smooth and shining as if they had just been bought. There wasn't a dent left in them and the green verdigris had been polished away.

It was the women of the family, or we children, who went back with the well-polished copper items. Sometimes we got money, sometimes eggs, a hen, a sack of potatoes or a broken pot as payment. We mended the pot and sold it in the next village.

Household utensils were often made of copper in those days. Copper has a way of becoming coated with verdigris, green and poisonous to people and animals. Therefore the inside of the copper vessels

My cousin, Solomia, and her husband retinning a kneading-trough for a bakery.

Muři vara e Solomia ai lako řom hanon jekh basina katar jekh pekarnia

Ande le špiti, polkuria ai traxtiria čirevenas o xabe ande bare tokatsia xarkune. Trobulas defial mišto vužarde kaste te na vilinin le manuš.

Kai le masaria amblavenas le mule žigenjen ande bare gančuria xarkune ando čardako, ai vi kai le pekarni sas le vasuria xarkune. Ai sa kadia vi kai la biariaki fabrika! Kotse sas le bare išturi kai žjalas miji litri biaria andre. Jekh data o berš nadjarenas avri e biaria anda le išturia, ai atunči akharenas le řomen te hanon le.

Copper-smithing and tin-plating

were covered with a thin layer of protecting tin. The tin was heated until it melted and was spread over the copper.

In hospitals, military barracks and restaurants the food used to be prepared in large copper boilers. They needed careful maintenance so that people weren't poisoned.

In the slaughter-houses there were dead animals hanging on large copper hooks from the ceiling, and in the bakeries they would use copper utensils, too.

Dad tinning with his brothers-in-law. One of the children is handling the goat's skin bellows. They are used for blowing air on the fire to make it burn evenly.

Muřo dad hanol peske šugorontsa, Jekh anda le glati phurden ande vindza kai sas kerdi anda murči bakreski, Kudolasa kerelas o manuš barval pe jag te šai phabol e jag vurta ai jekh fialo.

Muřo dad butivar kerelas buči hanomaski kai jekh fabrika biariaki paša Odenplan ando Stockholmo. O mui le ištungo kadia de činořo sas ta trudno sas jekh baro manuš te nakhel andre.

Muřo dad lelas pesa muře duie mai phure pralen le Vošos ai le Vilhelmos. Sar sas o Vilhelm mai činořo tsonas les te žjal andre mai anglal. Muřo dad inkerelas e skara žipo o Vilhelm vužarelas o ištu andral čišaiasa ai zarzaresa.

Pala kudo avelas e vriama te hanon arčičesa. Atunči anklelas vi o Vošo andre. Vo lelas pesa e lampa le gazoski, arčiči, ai dirzi. Akana vuže avelas e bari buči, ke musai sas te phiraven o arčiči mišto katargodi ande kudo baro ištu.

Trudno ai darani buči sas kudia. O arčiči trobunas te bilaven les kotse andre la lampasa, ai den tume gindo ke o arčiči mai phabardo lo katar o pai o čirado. Onivar pečalas kudo phabardo arčiči pe lenge vas, ta sa besiča kerdjolas pe lenge vas.

Kana sas e buči gata lelas muřo dad angle peski kniška bučaki. Kotse ramolas o xazaino (o rai la fabrikako) sar plačales e buči ai sodi love da ka muřo dad. Bištaipanž finiča pe kudia vriama ando 1930- laše sas pe jekhe djeseski buči.

Pa Vošo ai o Vilhelm či ramolas khanči. Numa muřo dad ingerda le ka jekh kafanava, kudia kniška laši sas leske kana phirelas ando gav pala buča.

Me naštivas te dikhav o hanomos ai melale tigei, dareš či kamavas te pašov paše. Sar lenas pe te keren jag muře pral te hanon, me strazom našavas ande tsera te garadjov.

Muřo dad sas zoralo amentsa, numa nas čořo vai jagalo. Šoha či marelas amen, ai barilam šai phenes bi čingarako vai xoliako. Ame pačasas o mui ai kerasas amari buči so sas amenge phendo, ai pala kudo samas libro te keras so ame kamas ai so si amenge drago. Sostar daralas muřo dad sas ke či kamelas te phiras čoře gažjentsa kai šai sičaren amen dilimos ai te na mai pačas o mui.

Not to mention the breweries! There they had copper tanks holding several thousand litres of beer. Once a year the beer was tapped off when the tanks were to be cleaned and tinned. Then they sent for a Gypsy.

My father used to do tinning for a brewery near Odenplan in Stockholm. The openings on top of the giant beer tanks were so narrow a full-grown man had difficulty crawling into it.

My father took along my older brothers, Vosho and Wilhelm. Wilhelm, who was the smallest one, went first into the tank. My father would stand outside holding the ladder while Wilhelm scoured it clean on the inside with sand and hydrochloric acid.

When it was time for the tinning Vosho had to crawl inside too. He carried with him a blow lamp, tin and rags. Now the boys had to move around and cover all of the inside of the giant beer tank with molten tin.

It was hard and dangerous work. The tin was melted on the spot with the blow lamp and melted tin is hotter than boiling water. Sometimes it splashed so my brothers got ugly blisters on their hands.

When the work was done my father took out his account book. That's where the brewery director wrote down how the work had been done and how much my father had been paid. Twenty-five crowns for a day's work, that was good pay in the 1930s and, as a reward, Dad would take the boys to a café. He was always careful with the account book for he would need it the next time he went looking for a job.

I hated the tinning and I didn't want to go near the sooty pots. As soon as my brothers made a fire to melt tin I ran and hid in a tent.

Dad was strict with us kids but he wasn't cruel. We seldom got beaten and we grew up without nagging. We were obedient and paid attention to our chores and in between we had a lot of freedom. What worried Dad the most was that we would end up in bad Swedish company and learn bad things and disobedience.

ŠOVTO ŠERO

O tivoli

Žipo le murš vurtonas piria ai hanonas žjanas le řomnia te drabaren. Numa e riate savoře ande jekh tsan žutisas ka tivoli.

– Le love či našen pe tute, phenelas muřo dad butivar, numa tu trobul te našes pala lende.

Muřo dad lape la feriasa (tivoli) strazom pala pervo marimos. Pervo činda jekh skafidi kai šai del puške o manuš. Pala kudo činda řata-lilengi, porme skafidi kai sikavelpe le naiesa, kai šudelpe menča, ai řatitsi, kai čirdelpe o šelo, kai šudes te phiren panž finiča, stena kai khelel o manuš ai grastoře kai den kulo.

Čačes ke trobulas but žutimos katar šiave, kak, bibia, veri, ai šlogi, te šai žutin muře dades ai dea.

Oni anda le mašinki la feriake čindam anda Niamtso. Oni kaver manglam po zakazo anda Švedo, numa le mai but mašinki kerdam korkořo anda vas.

Muřo pral o mai phuro o Fardi sas ando Niamtso ta sičilo te phiravel e řata le lile ngi. Kotse khelenaspe pe bare love! O mai čiřa kai šai tsolas o manuš sas bištaipanž finiča, ai o mai but kai šai nerilas o manuš sas deš kroni. Kudo sas pašti sa kadia but sodi nerilas jekh šloga ande dopaš šion.

Kai skafidi le menčengi šiudelas o manuš menči ande nange kutiji kai bešenas opral pa jekh avreste sar pyramidi. Le kutiji čindam le katar jekh fabrika tele ando Švedo, von tsonas goroxo andre. Ame tsasas po jekh bař ande svako kutija mai anglal sar te tsas o fedevo

CHAPTER SIX

The fairground

While the men were working with the coppersmithing and tinning the women went around telling fortunes. In the evenings we all looked after the fair.

"Coins don't come rolling towards you," Dad used to say. "You have to run and catch them."

Dad started with the fair right after the end of the First World War. First, he bought a shooting gallery. Then he got the Wheel of Cards, a booth with Point-at-a-Card, ball throwing and ring-throwing, Pull-the-string, rolling a five cent coin, an open air dance-floor and merry-go-rounds.

It certainly took many sons, uncles, aunts, cousins and hired hands, as well as grandfather and my mother to take care of everything. We bought some of the fairground attractions in Germany. Others we ordered in Sweden but we built most of them ourselves.

My oldest brother, Fardi, had been to Germany and learned how to look after the Wheel of Cards. There was big money at stake there! The lowest stakes were 25 cents and the first prize was ten crowns. That was almost a fortnight's wages for a farm-hand at the time.

The ball throwing kiosk meant throwing balls at a pyramid of empty tin cans. We bought the cans from a pea conserving factory in Skåne. We put a stone in every can before we closed the lid, or else the cans would have fallen almost just by

(left) Who dares to follow me into the deep sea?

Kon tromal te avel pala mande ando fundo la marjako

(right) We are enjoying ourselves and are often in the swing

opral, te na niči sas te pheren tele ferdi te čegosardanas pelende. Le bař mai kerenas jekh djela mišto, ke bašonas le kutiji zorales kana perenas.

Le menči suvasas korkořo. Šinasas jekh poxtan luludjantsa ande trin koltsura. Pala kudo suvasas ande jekh tsan o poxtan ai tsasas šelia andre.

Kudo kai šudela le menči ai peravelas numa jekh kutia, nerilas jekh karandašo vai jekh gumma kai lelpe tele ramomos. Kon sas mai baxtalo nerilas jekh kniška pa čor ai raibare. Te peravelas o manuš sa e pyramida le kutijengi atunči nerilas o manuš jekh nangi gažji anda vařo bare čučantsa. Savoře pařonas te nerin kasaviatar gažji kaste tson la ande pengo skafo.

The fairground

aiming at them. Besides, the stones made a noise when the tins fell. We sewed the balls ourselves. First we cut out triangles of decorated cloth. Then we sewed the balls together by hand and filled them with sawdust and cloth. Whoever threw the balls so that just one tin fell won a pencil or a rubber. If you were

Roundabout with hanging chairs in Kivik market 1949.

Karusela skaminorentsa po bazari Kivik ando berš 1949.

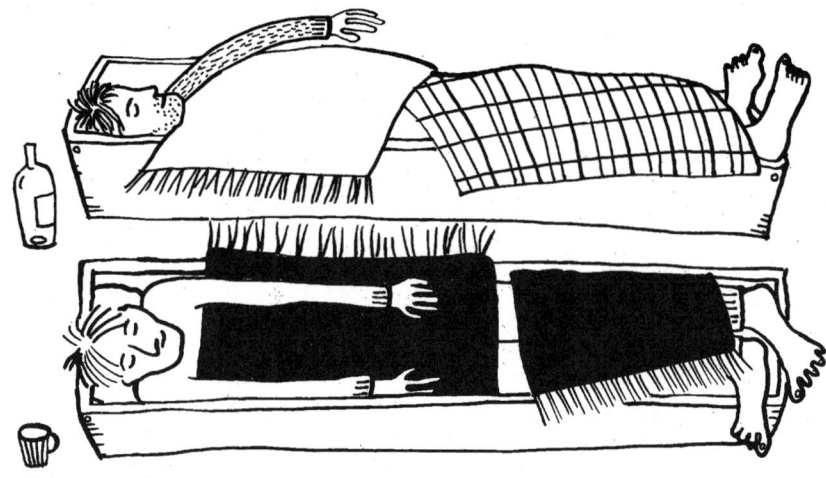

O šelo kai čirdelas o manuš sas le glatenge ai le žjuvljange, kotse nerilas o manuš papušiči. E skafidi kai šudelpe řati, sas maladi sakoneske kotse nerilaspe rišoře ai žjukela anda porselana.

Onivar musai sas mange te bešav ka skafidi kai šiudelpe panž feniča. Te šai kerdjolpe kudo khelimos trobul jekh skaterka kai si kvadratsi opral te šai ramol o manuš le numeria andre, ai trobul jekh skafidi ai jekh činoři truba kaštuni katar nakhen le panž feniča.

Svako panž feniča kai tsosas keresas te perel anda kudo šantso kaštuno, te perelas e palianka pe jekh trinali, nerisas trin po panženge, te perelas pe duiali nerisas deš feniča, te perelas pe jekhali atunči lesas palpale či panžengi kai tsodan. Numa mai butivares perelas e panžengi pe jekh vurka, atunči či nerilas khanči o manuš.

Kado khelimos defial drago sas butenge, numa mange nas. Mange nas drago ke svako riat kai keravas buči kotse, sa zeleno kerdjonas muře naja, sostar ke le love sas xarkune ai mukenas kokliala.

Mai drago sas mange vuže kana tsonas man te bešav ka skafidi kai sikavelas o manuš le najesa, kotse barim simas vužo ai aliaravas man raikano. Kotse sas patretsi pa šukar žjuvlia astarde karfiořantsa pe jekh phal anda mazonito. Kudia djela kerelas dopaš krono te sikaves pe gažjořa jekhe

The fairground

luckier you got a detective story. If you managed to make the whole pyramid fall you won a statuette of a nude woman with big breasts. Everybody longed to put her on top of their sideboard.

Pull-the-string was for women and children, there you could win dolls. The ring-throwing was fine for everybody, there you could win teddy bears and porcelain dogs.

Sometimes we arranged a Gypsy wedding to further amuse our audience at the fair. Then we charged two crowns entrance fee and we dressed up a young girl as a bride. We would dance and sing and sprinkle holy water over the bridal couple. It was quite a rowdy party. Then we repeated the pretend wedding in the next village. Sometimes we arranged Gypsy trials too. Here you can see my relatives performing for the TV in Malmö.

Onivar kerdjovasas te keras abiav kaste te plačal mai but le gažjen o tivoli. Kudo djes lasas počin dui kroni ando vudar ai vuriavasas jekha ternia šeja te avel e terni le abiaveski. Gjilabasas ai khelasas ai šiudasas pai svinto pe le terne. Čači gulania žjalas. Ai kadia kerasas gav gavestar. Onivares kerasas vi krisa řomane butom. Katka po patreto muře niamuri keren filmo po tv.

 Sometimes I had to take care of the Roll a Coin kiosk. You needed a check oilcloth for that, with numbers written in the squares, a table and a

lungo kaštesa. Pe zeja le patretoske ramolas te nerisardan vai niči.

E mai bari djela kai šai nerisas, sas jekh statua vařuni pa amperatiasa anda Egypto e Cleopatra. Numa te na gindin ke vušoro šai nerinas la, ke sa le gažje sikavenas le kaštesa pe patretsi kai nas but gada pe raklia, ai kotse kheladjonas von ke kotse šoha nas le numeria kai nerilpe!

Kudola djeli kai nerilas o manuš čindam le katar jekh taliano, kai phirelas gav gavestar la matorasa te bičinel djeli šukarimaske but kutora. Te činelas muřo dad 20 žjukela vařoske, 30 patretsi rakliantsa ai 10 Kleopatri šai linosas sa kudia partida pe jekh šelaki.

Me ačaravas man sar jekh rai kana phiravas kotse po tivoli jekhe parne nosovikosa ande posoči le kolineski.

– Naštin varekon te kerel limalo anda kudo raikano šiavořo? prasanas ma muře veri.

Von xoliariko sas ke me bešavas pe jekh šeran paša muři dei ande kasa, mai bine sar te žutiv len ando tivoli.

Kai karusela le skaminořengi trobulas o mai čiřa šov zorale glati. Von trobulas te našen ai te den kulo jekh kaš kai žjalas ande trošuleste tela e karusela, ai so mai zorales našenas ai denas kulo mai zorales žjanas kudola skaminořa ande barval.

Kanagodi kola kerdjolas angla kudia karusela. Ande jekh kola bešenas glati kai sas te anklen, ai ande kaver kola bešenas kudola kai sas te spiden. Kudo kai spidelas trivares mukenas te anklel jekh data ivja.

E riate muře pral denas drom sa le glaten kai nas řomane. Kal deš časuria avelas o raibaro, ai te dikhla sas ka jekh raklořo vai rakloři kotse, atunči muřo dad trobulas te počinel štrafo.

Mai sas jekh karusela kai bušolas krinolinen. Kudia defial šukar sas. Paša kudia krinolinen sas jekh radio baro kai žjalas e djili "O sole mio" ai vi kaver talianiska djilia.

Numa sas jekh karusela kai bušolas o čermo le šaxesko, pe kudia pařonas te anklen kudola kai sas kamade. Anda kudo ke pe jekh

small wooden grooved slide. Every five-cent piece at stake was rolled down the groove and if it landed on number three you won three five-cent coins, if it landed on a square with number two, ten cents, if it landed on number one you got your stakes back. Most of the time the five-cent piece fell on a line and then you didn't win anything. Rolling the five-cent piece was very popular, but I didn't like it. My hands were all green after a night there, because as the five-cent coins were made of copper my fingers also got so darned coated with verdigris.

Me, I'd rather look neat and flirtatious and stand around at the Point-at-a-card booth. Fastened with pins on a piece of slate board were postcards with beautiful ladies. It cost 50 cents to point at the ladies with a long stick. At the back of the postcards you could tell if there was a prize or not. The top prize was a plaster figure of the Egyptian queen, Cleopatra. But she was hard to win, because the men pointed only at the most scantily clad women, and they were almost always blank! We bought the first prizes from an Italian commercial traveller who came by car and sold fancy goods wholesale. If Dad bought twenty plaster dogs, thirty busty ladies and ten Cleopatras he could get them all for a one-hundred-crown note.

I was a really smart young gentleman who went around the fair with a white handkerchief in my breastpocket.

"Can't anybody make that elegant kid snivel a little?" my cousins teased me.

They were cross with me because I got to sit on a cushion next to Mum at the cash desk instead of helping with the merry-go-rounds. You needed at least six strong kids for the merry-go-round with its swings. They had to run round and round and push four logs arranged in a cross under the merry-go-round. The faster the kids ran the higher the swings flew. There was always a queue in front of the merry-go-round. One queue with kids to ride it and one queue with kids to push it. If you had pushed three times you could have a ride for free.

In the evening my brothers sent home all the kids who weren't Gypsies. At ten the police sergeant arrived and then Dad had to pay a fine if there were any Swedish children left at the fair.

Another roundabout was called the Crinoline. It was fascinating. Next to the Crinoline there was an automatic barrel-organ playing *O sole mio* and other Italian love songs.

But it was the Caterpillar that was the favourite for courting couples.

data anklelas avri jekh baro poxtan ai tsolas pe opral ta garavelas savořen pe kudia karusela. Atunči kerdjolas e djela romantiko! Sa le kamade ažukerenas pe kudia djela ke atunči šai čumidenas pe bi te dikhen le khonik.

So perelas tele o kham strazom kamavas te žjav te tsama tele ando vurdon. Me daravas katar o tuniariko ai vi katar le čuxane. Numa nas butivar kai žjasas te peras tele mai anglal sar le dešudui, vai bare vai glati sa kadia pozno sovenas. Savoře ande jekh data žjanas te soven, kon ande vurdona kon ande tseri.

Le šlogi sovenas ande jekh tsera kotse paša e skafidi le puškengi. Kotse sovenas von tsapeia sar le karfia ande duie meteronge jaštikuria. Kana tradasas tsasas le tseri ande kudola bare jaštikuria.

Le šlogi sas gažje švedaia kai nas le buča, ai phirenas kai ingerel le o drom, oni anda lende sas kasavendar kai roden mai čirado ai vojako trajo, ai oni sas frandukaria (kořovetsia). Von lenas fersavi buči ferdi te denas le čiřa xabe ai love řičijake. Muři dei šoha či mukelas len ando vurdon, ke penke žuva si le.

Mai anglal sar te žjas te sovas piasas čajo. Atunči tsolas pe muři dei te djinel le love katar e kasa ai čidelas le love katar le kaver kai kerenas buči kai le karuseli, kai le puški ai le but skafidia. Nas baro kontrolo pe love. But žjene garavenas peske jekh krono dui ande posoča, numa nas bari djela kudia.

Me kai simas o mai činořo šiav sovavas ando vurdon muřa deiasa ai dadesa. Vi muře kaver bi ansurime pral sovenas kotse, numa le ansurime pralen sas le lenge tseri ai lengi poriatka.

Muři dei mai suvda jekh kotor tsera ande tsera, kudo bušol pologo, kudo pologo suvda les voi anda sani selia ai tsoda čukeria kai bešenas šukar opral pa lengo tsan. Kadia sas le mai miro kana kamenas te aven korkořo.

Me sovavas pe phuv, vulojime ande dui perini luludjantsa, jekh opral ai jekh telal. Le perini sas tsule ai kovle ai pherdo anda mai laše por.

Kana savoře tsodepe te soven ande pača atunči mudarelas muřo dad e lampatka le karasinuski kaste avel tuniariko. Numa mai anglal sar kudo kerelas peske trošol angla amare řusiska ikoni ai řodjilaspe eta kadia:

– Le sama katar le činoře glati.

Atunči či mai daravas katar o tuniariko.

Suddenly, a giant folded cloth unrolled all over the Caterpillar. It was time for romance! All the couples on the roundabout were prepared and just waiting to disappear under the cloth so they could kiss.

As soon as the sun set I wanted to go inside the caravan. I was fearful both of the dark and of ghosts. But we rarely went to bed before midnight and there was no difference between children and adults, they all mixed together in the tents and wagons.

The hired hands slept by themselves in the tents where we kept our shooting gallery. They laid down as straight as nails in two metre long packing cases. When we travelled the marquee was packed in those cases. The hired hands were Swedes, unemployed men, adventurers and drifters who wandered along the road. They took any job as long as they got food and a little money for brandy. They were never allowed into our caravan, Mum said they had lice.

Before we went to bed at night we had tea. Then my mother counted the money from the box-office and collected coins and notes from those who took care of the merry-go-rounds, shooting gallery and booths. The control wasn't very strict. Putting a few coins in one's own pocket was called to 'garra' in Romani and everybody did it.

Me, being the youngest brother, slept in the caravan with Mum and Dad. My unmarried brothers slept there too, the married ones had their own tent and household.

My mum had sewn a canopy of thin silk cloth decorated with pompoms hanging over her and Dad's sleeping space. That was a way for them to get a little privacy. I slept on the floor, with two feather quilts with a flower pattern around me, one on top of me and one under me. The quilts were thick and soft and filled with the finest elder feathers.

When everyone had settled in the wagon Dad turned down the paraffin lamp so it was dark. Before that he made the sign of the cross in front of our Russian icons and prayed:

"Take care of the small children!"

Then I wasn't afraid of the dark any more.

EFTATO ŠERO

Muři dei

E pervo djela kai keravas kana uštavas sas te lav le kaltsi pe mande sar mai fugo. Jekh baro šiav řomano nas slobodo (voja) te sikavel pe ande sostia jekha žjuvliake, dareš či peska deiake. Vi o gad lavas pe ma strazom sar uštavas.

Kana simas getome atunči čidavas o tsan ai garavavas les opre pe jekh skafo ando kultso.

Kana me uštavas muři dei vuže uštadisas ai vi čirada čajo ando samovari pe veranda.

Makar ke me simas ternořo sa voi či phirelas bi dikhlesko angla ma. Či serav te dikhlem muřa da vai muře šogoritsi bi dikhlesko. Onivar kam maladjolas ke dikhav len sar vulaven le bal vai xalaven o šero atunči strazom čipinas:

– Ambolde tu inčal!

Atunči žjavastar kotsar lažiavesa, te dikhes jekha žjuvlia bi-dikhlesko bari djela sas atunči.

Angla vurdon sas muřa da jekh skafo pavusko. Kotse maškar o pavo tsolas voi o xabe.

– Xaladan le vas! pušelas voi kana dikhelas ke avav.

Nas voja khonik te asbal o manřo melale vastentsa.

Sas řom čoře pe kudia vriama, numa amen kana godi sas amen te xas. Vi kana sas o duito marimos ame xasas parno manřo ai mas lundjardo, šunko ai peredetsi diminiatsi čajosa. Musai sas te avel čil po manřo, ai na margarina. Le řom nai xanžvale po xabe!

O xabe xasas e riate. Atunči šukar sung sas pe antrego bar. Svako familia čiravelas peski piri xabe, numa katar svako tsera vai vurdon ašundjolas:

CHAPTER SEVEN

Mum

The first thing I did when I woke up in the morning was to pull on my trousers. An almost grown up Gypsy lad could not show himself in his underpants to any woman not even to his own mother. The shirt had to be on, too, before I got out of bed. When I was dressed I folded up my eiderdowns and piled them in a corner of the caravan.

Usually Mum had been long awake and had already made tea in the samovar on the veranda. Although I was really just a kid she never showed herself barehearted to me. I can't remember ever seeing my mum or any of my sisters-in-law without a headscarf.

If I accidentally surprised any of them while they were combing or washing their hair they shouted at me straightaway:

"Turn around!"

Then I went off shamefaced – to see a woman bare-headed was like her showing herself naked.

Mum had her cold store outside the wagon. That's where she kept the food amid blocks of ice.

"Have you washed your hands?" she asked me when I came in.

No one was allowed to touch the bread with dirty hands.

There were poor Gypsies but there was always food in my family. Even during the Second World War we used to have white bread with salted meat, ham and tomatoes for breakfast. And on our bread we would have butter not margarine. A Gypsy isn't stingy with food!

We had dinner in the evening. Then lovely smells would spread through the camp. Every family cooked for themselves, but from tents and wagons came the shouts:

– Aven ai xan! Den vareso ando mui!

Ame le glati našasas pe sa e bar ka bibi Olga zumavasas gulasch, zumi kainjaki galuškentsa kai bibi Belka ai sarmi kai řoza. Ame xasas ande trin štar tsana. Ande svako tsera čiravenas mai but xaben so lenga familia trobul.

Le slogi ai le bučaria xanas korkořo paša skafidi le puškengi. So sas mišto sas ke savořen sas le te xan ai čailonas. Te si ke ašelas xabe šiudasas les, či garavasas khanči po kaver djes. Ke darasas katar e mel ai o nasfalimos.

Mum

Mum as a newly married bride in Russia around 1900. All married women wore a headscarf in those days. Mum had silver coins bound into her long braids. The necklace was made of dollar coins and amber pearls.

Muři dei kana sas nevi ansurime karing o berš 1900. Sa le ansurime žuvlia phiravenas diklo, pe kudia vriama. Ande peske lundji čungi khovelas galbi rupone muři dei. Lako lantso sas kerdo anda galbi dolaroske ai perli.

"Please come inside and eat! Enjoy your meal!"

We children ran around and tasted goulash at Aunt Olga's, chicken soup with dumplings at Belka's and stuffed cabbage at Roza's. We had dinner in three or four places. In all the tents more food was cooked than what was needed to feed the families.

The 'lice-ridden' hired hands had to eat by themselves by the shooting gallery but everyone got food and ate until they were satisfied. If there were left-overs we threw them away. Nothing was kept for the next day. We were afraid of dirt and disease.

OXTOTO ŠERO

O khelimos

Kana mai barilem atunči mangle ma muře pral te djilabav lentsa ande orkesta. O Josef djilabelas ande garmunia o Vošo ande lauta ai o Folke bašavelas le dubi vo barilo ande lende. So mai trobulas le ande orkesta sas jekh kai djilabel ando kontrabas.

Naštivas te dikhav kudo kontrabas! Muře vas nas kerde te bašaven ande zorale sirmi sastrune. Pe muře naia kerdjonas bešiča kai pařadjunas ta dičolas o mas lolo tela murči.

– Šoha čimai ankliava pe stena! vačivas ma ka muři dei ai rovavas.

Voi phandelas mange čipti pel naia ai porme pale musai sas mange te djilabav. Musai sas te sičov la dokasa. Nas man karing musai sas mange te asav ai te kerdjuvav ke radoime sim makar ke le naia pečan rat.

Muřo čačo radoimos sas o khelimos. Jo, o khelimos sas muřo trajo! Me barilem pe stena le kelimaski, žjanavas te khelav mai anglal sar te phirav.

Muři dei, muřo phuro pral o Wilhelm ai me kerasas xoro ande jekh tsan. Anda gor lelaspe muři dei ai khelelas řusiska. Voi sičili te khelel ando S:t Petersburg ai ande Moska. Pala kudo lelape o Wilhelm te khelel čičutki.

Pala dui vai trin djilia, manas řavda le gažen numa čipinas:

– Akana kamas te dikhas le šiavořes! Anen le šiavořes! O šiavořo!! O šivořo!!!

Me bešavas pala stena ai ažukeravas, numa nas mange slobodo te avav angle mai anglal sar te bašavel o Folke ande le dubi zorales te kerel semno.

O, Devla če mišto sas mange atunči meravas dragostar kana avelas kudia vriama! E stena, e muzika le litriča, o publiko! Me simas vuriado

CHAPTER EIGHT

Dancing

When I had grown out of my short trousers my brothers insisted on my being part of the orchestra at the fair. Josef played the accordion, Vosho the violin and Folke had learned the drums. They needed a double-bass player in the band.

How I hated that double-bass. My hands weren't made for hard metal strings. My finger tips got blistered so the pink flesh appeared shining and unprotected.

"I'll never go on stage again," I complained and cried to my mother.

She put sticking plaster on my fingers and then I had to go on playing. It was supposed to make me tough. All I could do was look musical and happy although my fingertips were bleeding.

As for me it was dancing that made me happy. Yes, dancing was my life! I grew up on the dance floor of the fair and I could dance before I could walk straight. Mother, my elder brother, Wilhelm, and I used to perform together. Our show started with mother's Russian dances. She had learnt them in St Petersburg and Moscow. Then Wilhelm did his tap dancing.

After a few songs the audience got impatient and started shouting.

"Now we want to see the boy. Get the boy! The boy! The boy!'

I stood waiting behind the scenes but I couldn't make my appearance until Folke did a loud drum roll.

Oh God, how I loved that moment. The stage, the music, the spotlights, the audience. I used to wear a red silk shirt, wide black trousers and Russian boots with heels. I could have gone on dancing all night, my fear of the dark disappeared as the hours slipped by.

ande jekh lolo panřuno gad, ai kale bufle kaltsi ai bare řusiska kheria kuriasa. Šai kheldemas sořo riat, vi muři dar katar o tuniariko bilalas ai vi le časuria bilanas.

Jekh riat, kudo sas ando Skurup, avilo jekh raibaro kai lel sama.

– Te ašiaves o khelimos pe jekh data akana! phenda vo. O šiavořo musai te sovel pe kadala časuria. Opral pa le deš si akana. Te na pačana o mui si te dav tumen štrafo ke tson glaten te keren buči!

Ce baro zavarimos anklisto! O publiko čipilas muři dei čipilas.

– Sar te keras anda šiavořo! Ame avilam pala o šiavořo! čipilas o narodo.

– Buči le glaten! čipilas muři dei. O Aljoša 14 beršengo lo, vo činořo lo ai skurto ta gindin ke glata lo!

Numa me čačimasa simas deše beršengo, numa sosi anda kudia? Me pařovas te khelav ai kon šai phenelas ke nai muře čače berš? Pe vurma manas les karing musai sas o raibaro te kerel pe publikosko.

– Apo muken žjal! čipilas vo mai zorales katar le kaver, muken khelel o šiavořo. Mukav te khelel, ke sa nai raklořo švedano.

Ai pe bax ke mukla o raibaro, ke sa o narodo sas te maren pe.

Dancing

One night – it was in Skurup – the police sergeant came for his inspection.

"Stop dancing straightaway," he ordered. "The boy must go to bed. It's past ten o'clock. If you don't obey you'll have to pay a fine for using child labour."

What a fuss there was! The audience was yelling and Mum was yelling.

"But the boy, we've come here for the boy," yelled the audience.

"Child labour!" – shouted my mother. "Alyosha is fourteen years old. He's just short for his age."

My Uncle Bumba is dancing with my sisters-in-law. My older brother, Josef, furthest to the right, is wearing my mother's silver belt.

Muřo kak o Bumba khelel muře šogoriskentsa. Muřo pral o mai phuro o Josef tumna pe čači rig phiravel muřa daki rupuni kuštik

I was probably not much older than about ten at the time but what difference did it make. I loved to dance and who could prove how old I was? Finally, the police sergeant had to give up.

"All right, he shouted, trying to shout louder than anyone else." Let the boy dance. It's all right. After all, he's not Swedish."

Luckily this stopped the whole audience from starting a fight

ENJATO ŠERO

Drabarimos

Makar ke lavas sama katar muře vas sa me lem tele dopaš anda muřo nai o baro kana šinavas kaš jekh djes kurkesko. Kudo nai kai šindem či žutisarda man te na mai djilabav ando kontrabas, numa barim čimai trobulas te hanov. Anda kudia mai bine žjavas muřa deiasa te drabarel.

Muři dei drabarelas ando vas, ande lila ai ande boštiji kafake. Lake mišto sas ke avav lasa ande khera kai streia manuš. Me gindiv ke čiřa xaj sas lake korkořo.

Le mai but gažje sas laše ai dumolia, numa oni mukenas le žjukelen pe amende kana dikhenas ke řom sam.

Onivar maladjolas ke le gažjořa ando gavořo akharenas muřa da te piel lentsa kafa, kaste te phenel lenge pa kamimos ai romantiko djeli. Vi love ai vi glati kamenas te avel le ando trajo. Čiřa dragostia. Ai but bax.

Me bešavas miro pe jekh skamin paša o vudar ai ažukeravas. Te sas laše manuš denas man pirožna.

Defial mišto sas mange maškar le gaže! Dikhavas sar tson parne pištirutsia kai khosel pe o mui ai servisio kafako loludjantsa. Vi me kamlemas te avel amen kadia, te bešas ande jekh kher ai te avel amen loludja ande jekh piri. Me kamavas te avel man bania kai si pai ando kranto, ai te na mai pavo ma ando veš diminiatsi ai vi e riate.

Jekh iven kana sas o duito marimos, kadia but phirdem kai jekh familia ando Kristianstad ta kamenas te len ma peske te bariaren ma. Len nas le glati ai vi kam sas lenge mila mandar ke či phiravas ande škola ai nas amen či kher kai te bešas. O gazda le kheresko sas portnoi (kai suvel

CHAPTER NINE

Fortune-telling

Even though I took such care of my hands, I cut off half of my thumb one Sunday when I was chopping wood. That I was missing half a thumb didn't get me out of playing the bass in the fair orchestra but I did get out of the tinning. Instead, I could go with my mother when she did her fortune-telling. My mother told people their fortunes by the lines on their palm, with cards and coffee grounds. She liked to have me with her when she went round to other people's houses. She must have felt unsafe on her own. Most of the time people were pleasant enough but there were some who sent their dog out when they saw a Gypsy woman in the doorway.

Sometimes ladies would send for mother when they had a coffee party. They were longing to hear about love and romance. They also wanted money and children. A little excitement. Lots of happiness. I sat and waited silently on a chair by the door. If they were kind people, they sometimes offered me a biscuit.

How happy I was among the Swedes! I watched them lay the table with white serviettes and a flower-decorated coffee set. I wanted that too, to live in a house and keep geraniums in a pot. I wanted a bathroom with running water and no need to get my private parts frozen stiff in the woods in the morning and at night.

One winter during the Second World War I ran off so often to a family in Kristianstad that they wanted to adopt me. They had no children of their own and they must have felt sorry for me – a child who neither went to school nor lived in a house. The man of the family was a tailor and he sewed me a sailor suit which I got as a Christmas present.

ai lašiarel tsalia). Vo kerda mange tsalia ketaniska ai da le mange sar pudarka po krečuno.

Kai dinosas man muře niamuri pe gažje! Kana bilailo o iv atunči tradamtar mai angle, numa ži atunči mai da ma papuči lakoske ai vi jekh gad suvdo anda vas anda mai sano poxtan bombakosko.

Me dikhavas seloso pe le rakloře le gažjenge. Von miazonas ke trajin ande kaver lumia. Onivar vi davas man gindo, či trajin pra tasades? Nas lenge tristo? Ande muři lumia sas man o khelimos ai o libromos. Ai muře bare pral! Makar ke onivar prasanas man, me žjanavas ke von kamenas man čačes ai denas man sa so mangav.

Ferdi muřo pral o mai baro o Josef phirelas kai škola anda sa ame le glati. Vo korkořo alosardia te žjal ka škola, či žjanav sar avila leske kudo gindo. Sas les lašio šero djinimasko.

But my parents wouldn't give me away so easily. When the snow started melting we took to the road but not before I had been given patent leather shoes, too, and a shirt hand sewn from the finest cotton.

I watched the Swedish children enviously. They were living in a totally different world. But wasn't their world too narrow, I wondered. Weren't they bored? In my world there was dance and freedom. And my big brothers. Yes, they did tease me but at the same time they loved me and spoiled me.

In front of the tent together with my brother's children.

Angla muře daki tsera muře nepotontsa.

O Josef arakhadjilo baxtalo. Muři dei mai čiřa sas te merel kana arakhadjilo o Josef. Sa gelitar e zor anda late.

– Te si ke baxtalo san, si te trajiv phenda voi peske bebetoske.

Voi trajisarda ai o Josef anklisto lako mai řizgijime.

O Josef sas raikano sar mande. Kana godi sas šukar vuriado, sa kadia šukar ande škola sar vi pe stena ande orkesta. Vareso bročume te avilosas lesko parno gad musai sas strazom te tačarav e planča.

Sar aresasas pe jekh nevo tsan o Josef vuže žjalas te ramol pe kai škola. Me gindiv ke gelo ande mai but sar panžvardeš školi, vi djinelas so denas les khere te kerel ai vi ramolas svako djes pa pesko trajo. Leske sa jekh sas ande soski klasa tson les, leske numa sas bari buči te sičol.

Muřo Del če šukar ramolas vo lašio va sas les! Kana muřo dad dikhla sar vo ramol tsolas les te kerel le hertiji, le reklami katar o tivoli. Miazonas bari djela.

Mange mišto sas ke či žjavas ande škola. Kon sas te lel sama katar muře gugle tena avilemas khere po sořo djes? O činořo šošoi kai musai te dav les šax ai morkoja, ai e Vira muřo žjukel kai kana godi mangel te xarundav leske kan, le golomburia, e papin, o kokošo, e tutka ai le trin činoře niamtsiska kainja. Čačo parko žigenjengo sas man oni anda le žigenji dine ma ivja ai oni lem ando pařuimos katar le mužiča.

Či mai dikhlem kasavestar šošoj te merel te žjal katar godi ai te xal les griza katar godi. Sar aresasas ande jekh nevo gav vo strazom sungalas ai kerelas sar niči ai arakhelas o gavořo, ai či avelas khere žipo či čaliolas. Me inke či aliarav sar jekh činořo šošoj šai arakhel angle ai vi palapale te avel pe gora kai šoha nas!

Le šošojeske sas drago dumolia ai trazi manuš kai či pien řečia. Kana varekon xuliarelas les, vazdelas o punřo ai čindjolas pe. E bibi Olga ansurisaili jekhe zorale gažjesa. Vo vazdelas skamina peske dandentsa. Vo nas dumolo. Numa o šošoj khelavelas les! Kon xuliarelas le šošojes kheladjolas, ke čindjolas pe vurta pe leste!

E Vira muři žjukli sas jekh godjaver žjukli. Ande muře punře sas po sořo djes ai defial raikani ai řizgijime sas ta numa laše djeli xalas voi delikatess.

My big brother, Josef, was the only one of us children who went to school. It was he who wanted to go but I don't know where he got the idea from. He must have had a good head for learning.

Josef was born with a caul. That's what we call it when you are born with a piece of the afterbirth left on your head. Mum almost died at his birth. All her strength left her.

"If you are lucky I will live," she said to her baby son.

She lived and Josef became her favourite.

Josef was fussy like me. He was always nicely dressed, as neat at school as in the fair orchestra. I had to warm the iron if there was the slightest wrinkle on his white shirt.

As soon as we arrived in a new place Josef went to the nearest school and registered himself. He must have gone to more than fifty schools. He did his homework and also kept a diary. He didn't care which class the head teacher put him in a long as he got to study.

My God, what beautiful handwriting he had! When my father found that out Josef got to do the posters for the fair. They were real works of art.

As for me, I was only too happy not to go to school. Who would look after my darling animals if I was gone all day? Little Pelle, the rabbit, who needed cabbage and carrots. My dog, Vira, who wanted to be scratched behind her ears, the carrier pigeons, the duck, the rooster, the turkey and the three German bantam hens?

I had my own little zoo with animals I had been given as presents from farmers. Pelle was the most curious rabbit I had ever come across. As soon as we arrived in a new town he sniffed his way to where the market was and he didn't come back until he had had enough to eat. I never understood how a poor rabbit could find his way round in unknown places.

Pelle was fond of quiet and sober people. If anybody made trouble with him he lifted his leg and wee'd on them. Aunt Olga had married a so-called tooth athlete. He was a strong man who could lift chairs with just his teeth. But he couldn't handle Pelle. If you were bad to the rabbit you were hit by a jet of urine which always hit its target.

Vira was a wise miniature Doberman. She followed me around the whole day and was so spoiled

E tutka nas kadia raikani. Vo numa tsolas pesko šero paša muři buka ai bašelas kana sas bokhalo.

Le golomburia phirenas ande bar sar von kamen. Ratjako numa trobulas te vazdav muře vas karing o čeri, ai strazom avenas le golumburi ai bešenas pe muře vas.

Le kainja kai sas ame sas jekh vitsa činoři niamtsiska, lenge anře sas činoře sar menči katar pingpong.

E papin ai o kokošo anda gor sa mudarenas pe, numa pe vurma von sas le mai bare baratsi. Kadia bare vurtača ankliste ta le kokošos či mai xalas les griža kai le kainja, numa po sořo djes phirelas ande bar la papinasa ai kerelas barimata.

Sodi me kamavas muře žigenjen! Kana mučisas ame tsavas len ando kamiono. Muřo dad tradelas ai muři dei bešelas anglal lesa. Mai anglal sar te amboldel muřo dad e čaia ando kamiono, vazdavas fugasa o prezento ai tsavas le žigenjen andre, fersaves tsavas len ke sa ande graba samas.

– Te aven laše ai te bešen miro akana phenavas lenge me, trobul te řivdin tume žipo aresas angle.

Onivar bešenas le šlogi kotse ando tuniariko maškar le karuseli, tseri, belia, plaki ai skafidia. Atunči anklelas lenge kompania po drom, le žigenji ai le šlogi, te na gindin ke le šlogi mai vužile anda kudo.

she would only eat the best food. The turkey wasn't so snobbish. He would put his head on my cheek and cackle when he was hungry.

The carrier pigeons circled round the camp as they wished. At night all I had to do was lift up my hands to the sky and in a minute they came down and sat, one on each of my hands,

The bantam hens were German, their eggs were small and round like ping-pong balls.

How I loved my animals! When we were on the move they went in the truck. Dad would drive the vehicle and mother sat with him in the cab in front. Just before Dad turned the key in the ignition I would lift the tarpaulin and tuck away the animals inside. It was a bit of a mess because I had to move fast.

Be good and keep quiet, I told them. You can come out when we get there.

Sometimes a few of the hired hands were already inside in the darkness among the merry go rounds, poles, signs and booths. The hired hands would make the trip alongside the animals and that certainly didn't make them any cleaner.

DEŠTO ŠERO

O duito marimos

Me simas dešujekhesko vai dešudongo kana lape o duito marimos 1939. Le manuš sa ande dar sas, defial trudno sas ai but djeli sas kai manas amen. O kher le forosko vulavelas pe svako familia švedisko mešte hertiji, kai numa pe kudola šai činesas čil, kafa, zaro ai kaver xabenata. Numa sar amen le řomen nas amen domicilio (adresuria) ai či žjanasas dareš amare čače berš, trudno defial phares sas te šai las kasavendar hertiji xabeneske. Musai sas amenge te milujisame ai parke pe čangende te mangas ame te šai las jekh kasaviatar hertija pe amari bari familia.

Ande jekh djes ando Stockholmo čorde katar muři šogoritsa vi kudola zaloga hertiji kai dine la o kher le forosko. Voi pařolas xuliatar tsoda pe phuv ai numa čipilas. Bari buči kerdjila pe anda kudia djela. Le čores či mai arakhle, numa vi le gazeturia ai vi po radio phende pa la řomnaki mila ai nekazo anda lake glati. Pala kudia djela vuže tradenas amenge le gaže milatar kasavendar hertiji pa sa o Švedo. Le gažjořa kai kerenas buči kai le levči diliavonas sodi ame činasas.

Numa te phenas o čačimos voi numa xoxada ke čordela. Musai sas kasavendar djeli te kerel o manuš ke nas amen karing. Numa pe bax ke či žjangla muřo dad, ke atunči xale saste avas!

Ando marimos trudno sas vi te arakhas xarkuma ai arčiči kai amari buči. Či benzino naštilas te činel o manuš.

CHAPTER TEN

The Second World War

I was eleven or twelve years old in 1939 when the Second World War began. People were afraid, it was a time of crisis and a shortage of everything. Every Swedish family was given ration cards from the state in order to be able to buy butter, coffee, sugar and other food supplies. But we Gypsies who had neither fixed addresses nor any idea of our dates of birth, we had trouble getting any ration cards. We had to beg and plead for every little food coupon for our large families.

One day in Stockholm one of my sisters-in-law was robbed of the few coupons she had received from the Emergency Office. She went crazy and lay down in the street screaming. There was a great fuss about it. They never found out who the thief was but the papers wrote about it and the radio station told the story of the poor mother. Shortly afterwards generous people from all over Sweden were sending us ration cards. The grocery shop assistants were surprised when we went shopping for luxuries. In fact, the story about the robbery had just been made up. You had to act like that to get by. But if Dad had found out what really had happened he would certainly have been angry.

During the war it was hard to find copper and tin for our trade. Petrol wasn't available either. Our bumper cars did not move nor did the merry-go-rounds. They rusted away.

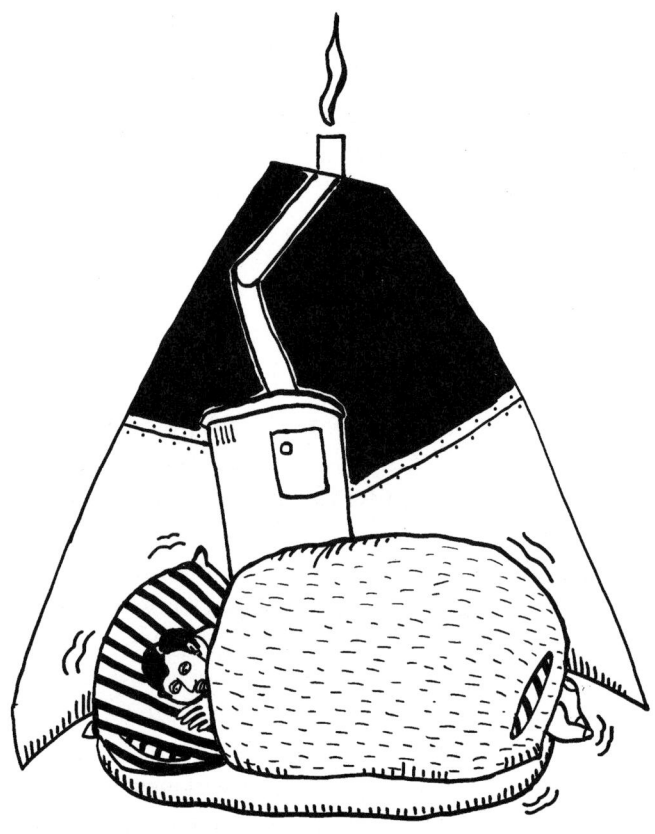

Amare matori sa ašiade sas po tsan, sar vi amare karuseli. Sa řužinisaile.

Le ivenda ando 40-berš defial zorale sas. Defial but iv delas, butivar sas karing le tranda graduria šil e riate. Musai sas amenge te phagas le steni le khelimaske te keras jag kana či arakhasas kaš.

O papo mulo, lesko gono (galav) nango, ai love manas.

O marimos žjalas ande le tsema paša amende, ai ame darasas ke kam aresel o marimos ži ando Švedo.

The Second World War

The winters in the early 1940s were very hard. The snow came down heavily and a temperature of −30°C at night wasn't unusual. Many of the open air dance floors were chopped up and disappeared into the stoves in the tents.

Grandfather had died, his Russian trunk was empty, there was no money left. The war raged in the neighbouring lands and we were afraid it would reach Sweden.

In front of the tent with my niece and nephew

Angla e tsera sim muře nepotontsa

Ande doba kana sas tumnia ando 1942 lam o dježes katar o Gjävle ži ando Stockholmo kaste te nakhavas kotse o iven. Amaro tivoli tsodam te žjal ande magazina jekh rig kai garavelpe djeli ai tovaro. Numa dikhen so maladjol kana avel o čořimos, o paravuzo le dježesosko kai žjalas po vapuro si les jekh bov, ai katar kudo bov xutel jekh skentija ži kai amaro vaguno kai sas amaro tivoli andre, ai kadia lape te phabol sa o vaguno ai vi amari feria.

Pašti sa amare djeli ai tovaro xasardam. Čači prikaza sas.

Čoři doba sas atunči, la amen o čořo vas ta vi o vurdon gelo ande sa kudia vriama. Akana phenav tumenge sar. Muřo dad arakhla jekhe gažjes kai ašilo lesa te čirdel leske o vurdon ži ando Gjävle, numa po drom kai žjalas maladjilo vi jekh raklo kai vurta kudo djes sas te ansurilpe ai žjalas ka pesko abiav ai kaste namai xal čino la ai tsodape te bešel pe řuda le vurdonesko ai po čořimos la ai pelo gero raklo tela vurdon ai mulo. Kadia muři dei či mai kamla te bešel ande kudo vurdon ta la muřo dad ai bičinda les.

Ai muře žigenji, či kamav či te dav man gindo pe lende. Oj Devla, če mila gere. E tutka, e řatsa, e papin ai le kainja sa xale le muře niamuri. Le golumbon line le le raibare.

Či mai ašiavas anda roimos kana davas man gindo ke šoha či mai dikhava le.

– Na mai rov, žjuvliořio! čipinas pe mande muře pral ai phenenas muřa dake.

– Kudo Aljoša, čo činořo šiav arakhadjilo sar jekh žjuvli!

In the autumn of 1942 we got on a train from Gävle to Stockholm in order to stay there during the winter. The amusement park was transported by a goods train to be stored for the winter, but the train was pulled by a steam locomotive and a spark from the firewood boiler set our wagons on fire. The amusement park attractions were burnt down.

We lost almost everything. Yes, that was a tragedy.

Our caravan was also lost that autumn. Dad had trusted a fellow to transport the caravan to Gävle. On the way a man came and sat on the towbar between the lorry and the caravan. He was happy and a little bit drunk and on his way to a wedding. Misfortune struck, the fellow fell off and landed under the caravan wheels. So, the future bridegroom was crushed. After that Mum would not have the caravan back.

As for my animals, I don't want to think about them. Oh, the brutes. Turkey, goose, duck and hens the family ate them all. The police took the pigeons. I couldn't stop crying when I realised I would never see them again.

"Stop crying, you woman!" grumbled my brothers and complained to our mother.

"That Alyosha, your youngest boy, you've turned him into a girl."

DEŠUJEKHTO ŠERO

Jekh nevo trajo ando Stockholmo

Ando Stockholmo laspe jekh nevo trajo. Akana nas ame či feria ai či vurdon.

Ame mučisailam ande jekh hotelo kai bešenas matrosuria ando purano foro. Muřo dad pučinelas panž kroni pe štar sobi svako riat. Ande mai bari soba bešelas muřo dad ai muři dei, me ai o Josef. O Wilhelm sas les jekh soba korkořo peska familiasa. Sa kadia sas vi ka o Folke ai leski řomni. Ande štarto soba bešelas o Voso peske šove šiaventsa ai peska řomniasa la Singoallasa.

Mange sas drago le pajaria (matrosuria) nas či jekh doš pe lende. Von sas dumolia ai ame samas lentsa dakordo. Numa von sas perdo žjuva! So si kadala pajaria, anenas le žjuva pe amende ando hotelo. So šai keras? Khanči. Ferdi te duriovas lendar ai te na hamis ame le gažentsa kai si melale.

Me ai muře šogoritsi samas mai but ande kuxnia. Lam ame ai khoslam sapuiesa na ferdi e phuv numa vi le ziduria ai vi o čardako. Le vasuri kai sa ande kuxnia či asbadam le, ame gelam ai čindam neve.

Kana sa e kuxnia vuži či mai muklam khanikas te aven andre, či le pajaria ai či le raklia le hoteloske.

– Marel le o Del, phenda muři dei, katse či aven andre! Lam amenge jekh čaia ai phandadam o vudar kai e kuxnia.

Me davas la raia xabe svako djes kaste te na asbal o bov.

– Nils Erik so lašiardan adjes? pušelas e rai svako djes. Lašiarde če šogoritsi kudalestar lašio čaio kai si fruti andre? Bangarelas o šero ai mangelas:

– Šai den man čera čaio?

CHAPTER ELEVEN

A new life in Stockholm

A whole new life began for us in Stockholm. Now we had neither fair nor caravan.

We moved into a shabby hotel for sailors in the Old Town. Dad rented four rooms for five crowns each a night. Dad, Mum, Josef and I stayed in the largest room. Wilhelm got a room of his own for his family and so did Folke and his wife. Vosho was staying with his six children and his wife, Singoalla, in the fourth room.

I liked the sailors, there was nothing wrong with them. They were honest people and we got along well. But the lice. The lice! These sailors, they brought both headlice and bedbugs to the hotel. What could we do? Nothing. Just keep our distance and not mix with the Swedes and their dirt.

My sisters-in-law and I took over the kitchen. First we scrubbed it with soft soap, not just the floor, but the walls and the ceiling too. We didn't even touch the household items and the pots of the hotel, we bought new ones. When the kitchen had been polished and was ready, neither the sailors nor the hotel maids were allowed inside.

"God damn it," Mum said, "this is it!" We got ourselves a key and locked the kitchen door.

I was cooking for the landlady every day, to keep her away from the stove.

"Nils-Erik, what about your food today? Did your sisters-in-law make that kind of nice tea with fruit in it?" She put her head to one side and pleaded:

"Is it possible to get a little glass?"

– Jo šai das tut čaio, phenasas ame, numa tu naštis te aves andre ande kuxnia te meliares.

Kana kamenas le pajaria te tačaren pai vai te čiraven kafa phenenas muře šogoritsi:

– Žjan ai pušen le šiaves kai si ande kaver soba, vo si kai purončil pe e kuxnia.

Numa šoha ando trajo či mukasas len andre! So te keren kotse te pheraven peske žjuva pe phuv ande kuxnia!? Lavas me lendar o pai ai čiravavas lenge kafa.

– Nai pačamos če vuže san tume le řom, phenda e rai le hoteloski. Kado me šoha či gindisailem.

– Numa akana žjanes, phendem me, ai phandadem o vudar ka e kuxnia.

My sister-in-law, Singoalla, fortune-telling in Stockholm.

Muřĭ šugoritsa e Singoalla drabarel ando Stockholmo.

"Yes it is," I answered, "but you cannot come into the kitchen and make it dirty."

When the sailors wanted to heat water and make themselves some coffee my sisters-in-law said:

"Go into that room and ask the boy, he's the one who's in charge of the kitchen."

But nope, never in my life! As if they could come inside the kitchen and make a mess! And drop their lice on the kitchen floor! I took their coffee pot from them and heated the water for them.

"Amazing how clean you are, you Gypsies,!" said the hotel landlady. "I never knew that."

"Now you know," I said, and turned the key to the kitchen door.

We belonged to the Orthodox church. The first thing we did when we came to a new place to stay was to put up our icons. They were placed in a corner. A little oil lamp burnt all the time next to them to light them up. Then we borrowed a sewing machine and Wilhelm sewed curtains and covers for worn-out furniture.

Ame samas anda khangeri ortodoks. E pervo djela so kerasas kana avasas ande jekh nevo kher sas ke tsasas opre amare ikoni. Tsasas le ande jekh kultso. Jekh činoři lampa vuloieski phabolas kana godi paša lende ai delas le vediaria. Porme lelas o Wilhelm jekh mašinka ai suvelas gardini ai nevo poxtan pe le mublori.

Tuniariko ai iven sas ando purano foro. Či o šionuto ai či o kham či areselas pe le tang vuliči. Me davas jag sa le letriča ando kher. Ma bi te žjanas onivar merenas sa le letriča ai kerdjolas sa tuniariko ande soba.

– Kon si kai mudarel? pušelas muřo dad. Gelo o plono? Žja ai dikh, Aljoša!

Numa či arakhavas či jekh doš.

Jekh djes kana šilavavas e phuv ande amari soba, dikhav sar jekh vas avel lokořes pa o vudar. Me šudem mandar e motora ai kerdem mange trušol angla le ikoni.

A new life in Stockholm

It was winter and dark in the Old Town. Neither the sunlight nor the moonlight reached the alleys. I switched on all the lamps in our rented rooms but even though none of us understood how, it usually turned pitch-dark in the rooms.

"Who is turning out the lights?" Dad asked. "Is it a fuse that's blown? Go and see, Alyosha!" But no, there was nothing wrong with the fuses.

One day when I was sweeping the floor in our room, I noticed a hand slowly passing the doorway. I threw the broom away and made the sign of the cross in front of our icons.

Many well-known artists painted my portrait. This one was done by an artist named Laraeus.

But vestume kai makhenas patretai makhle muřo patreto. Kado patreto makhla o Laraeus.

– Devla kai san baro ande čo čeri, te avel tuke mila anda mande! rudjisailem me.

Kana me bešavas angla amaro Del mulo sa o letriko ando kher. Atunči avilo mange jekh gindo. Lem e motura ando vas. Kana dikhlem o vas pe duito data dem jekh sa muřa zorasa. Kasko sas o vas gindis?

La raiako katar o hotelo, ke ratjako dikhlem sar sas lako vas phanglo. De katar kudo djes či mai mudardjilo o letriko.

Kana puterdjilo o milaj puterdem e feliastria le hoteloski ke kamavas te avel barval andre. O hotelo sas purano ai sas les felestri kai šai bešesas ai dikhesas po kham.

Jekh djes pušla man jekh gažjo kai nakhelas o drom:

– Manuša, kames te makhav jekh patreto pa tute?

Jekh šukar raikano manuš sas kai pušla man.

– Ai kon san tu? pušlem me.

– Me sim jekh manuš kai makhav patretsi, hajdi mantsa khere ai makhav jekh patreto pa tute, dava tu čera love.

Me šoha či ašundem pa jekh kasavatar djela ai kamavas te dikhav, o gažjo sas defial raikano ai man plačaia ma.

Kadia si kai me areslem ande kado kai makhen patretsi, ai bešavas modelo khere vi ka o Isaac Grünewald ai vi ka o prins Eugen.

Jekh data da man o Isaac Grünewald jekh patreto pa mande. Numa mange nas drago ai šindem les. Kudo kijisailem butivar ke dav man gindo če baro ai vestume manuš kai makhelas sas vo.

"Dear God in heaven," I prayed. "Have mercy!"

While I was standing there in front of Our Lord the lights went out. Then I got an idea. I got ready with the broom. The next time the hand appeared I hit it with all my strength. The very same night the landlady had a plaster on her arm and from then on we had lights in our room.

When the spring arrived I opened up the windows of the hotel rooms. I wanted to feel the fresh air. The sailors' hotel was old and had deep bays at the windows where I could sit sunbathing. One day somebody on the street talked to me:

"Young man, do you want me to paint your portrait?"

It was a handsome man who was asking.

"What kind of a man are you yourself?" I asked him back.

Me, 13–14 years old.

Katse sim 13–14 brešengo.

"I'm an artist," he said. "Come to my place and I'll paint your portrait. I'll give you some money."

I had never heard of anything like that but I was curious and I liked this fine man. He had the manners of a true gentleman.

That's how I came into contact with the world of art and I was a model both at Isaac Grünewald's studio and at Prince Eugen's.

Isaac Grünewald once gave me a drawing. But I thought he had made me so ugly that I tore it up. I've regretted that many times, when I realised what a fine and famous artist he was.

Von kai makhenas sas lenge drago te makhen ma ke me simas o šiav le birevosko pe le řom. Nas but tsemaria ando Stockholmo pe kudia vriama, anda kudo sas lenge drago te makhen patretsi pa mande, vi mande khere ai vi lende. Me nerivas laše love pe kado.

Nas phares te arakhes manušen kai kamenas te drabaren pe. Me phiravas ande le kafanavi ando Stockholmo ai phenavas:

– Lašio djes me sim řom, si varekon kai kamel te drabarelpe? Sikav mange čo vas ai me phenav tuke pa či bax. Ferdi dui kroni kerel. (Kudo sas sodi kerelas te žjan dui žjene ando cine.)

– Bre če interesno! čipinas le raklia kai servinas ai kai kerenas buči ande le levči. Ašiav ai drabar amen!

Le raklia dilaile kana ašunenas pa pengo trajo sar avela mai angle.

– Mai den ma čeřa love ai me žjav ka le murmunči ai kerav fermiči šoha te na mai avel pe tumende e prikaza. Von pačanas svako vorba kai me phenavas. Kudo kai phenavas pa le murmunči nas čačes, numa butivar phenavas o čačimos. Sar keravas či me naštiv te phenav.

Those artists, they were inspired when they painted my portrait, the son of a real Gypsy chief! Foreigners were rare in Stockholm at the time and so many artists wanted me to sit as a model, both at their studios and at the Academy of Arts. I earned quite a lot of money.

It was easy finding people who wanted their fortune told, too. I went around cafés and restaurants in Stockholm.

"Hallo, I'm a Gypsy," I said. "Do you want your fortune told? Show me your hand and I'll tell you your fortune. It's only two crowns." (That was almost enough for a ticket to the cinema, it cost two crowns and twenty cents)

"Oh, how interesting!" shouted the waitresses and shop assistants. "Stay around and tell us our fortunes!"

They got all excited when I told them about the love that was in store for them.

"Give me another coin and I'll go to the cemeteries and cast a spell so that you'll never have any more troubles," I continued.

They believed every word. I had made up that thing about the cemeteries, but I have actually told the truth many times while fortune-telling. How that happened, I can't even explain to myself.

DEŠUDUITO ŠERO

E bar ando Sköndal

Akana sas ando aprilo 1943. Amari familia naštilas mai te bešas ando hotelo le pajarengo. Bešasas ke či žjanasas kai te mučis ame.

Jekh devlikano manuš kai bušolas Sundberg ai o Sven Andersson kai sas konsulento pe le řom ažutinas ame. Kudola dui laše manuš ande amenge palia, čeri ai jekh kimpo ando Sköndal avrial o Stockholmo. Kotse kerda amenge jekh bar řomani.

Muře pral kerenas ramči ai tsonas poxtan opral. Anda mazunito kerenas ziduri ande čera. Muřo dad kerelas bova anda bidoja vulojeske, ai trubi kai denas avri anda e čera.

Ame kamasas te anzaras amari feria numa či mukhle amen ke pra paše sas le murmunči.

Lam ame te zumavas te hanosaras, numa či delas sa kači love sar mai anglal. O marimos kai sas ande lumia kerda ta but gažje daranas anda pesko lov. Nas le love či te gulain ai či te lašiaren peske vasuri.

Ame bešlam but berš ando Sköndal. Nas laše berš o trajo sa trudno.

Baro šil sas ande le tseri ai le kherořa. Ivende diminiatsi musai sas te šilavas o iv pa čardako mai anglal sar te keras jag.

O konsulento le řomengo sas tsodino katar o tsem kašte te ažutil amen. Vo anelas amenge poxtana te tsas opral pa le tseri te na del andre o iv ai o pai pe amende. Me keravas jag ande le bidoia le vuloieske numa ferdi jekh metro kruglom tačolas. Porme pale paholas. O pai ande le vedri kerdjolas paho ai le bal pahonaspe po šeran le ratja le ivendeske.

Porme areslo o nasvalimos ande bar. Muřa deiako mai lašio šav nasvailo ande čixotka. Kai daranas ke perdjon musai sas te tsas le činořes ande jekh kher glatengo. Kudo sas o Valodja, muře pralesko šiav.

CHAPTER TWELVE

The camp in Sköndal

Now it was April 1943. Our family couldn't stay at the sailors' hotel any longer. We were still there only because we didn't know how to get out of there. We had nowhere to go.

A religious man called Sundberg and an advisor on Gypsies called Sven Andersson came to help us. These two nice people got hold of wood, plywood, canvas and a place in Sköndal outside Stockholm where we could build a tented camp.

My brothers made wooden frames and covered them with canvas. The plywood was used for the walls. Dad made stoves out of oil drums, with pipes serving as chimneys pushed through the canvas.

We wanted to build up our fair there too but the authorities wouldn't let us do that. The camp was too close to the Forest Cemetery.

We could do tinning again but it didn't bring in as much money as it used to. The war in the outside world had caused many Swedes to be careful with their money. They couldn't afford either retinning their pots and pans or entertainment.

We lived in the camp in Sköndal for many years. They were not good years. We were going downhill. It was cold and damp in the draughty tents and huts. In the winter mornings we had to shovel the snow off the roofs before we could start making a fire.

The Gypsy advisor, Andersson, had been appointed by the state to help us. He rented tarpaulins which we put over our tents to keep out the snow and melted ice. I heated the oil heater until it was burning hot but the heat only reached one meter or so. Then came the frost. The water froze in the buckets and our hair froze to the eiderdowns during the frosty nights.

Our kind friends Sundberg and Andersson on a visit to Sköndal.

Amare laše manuš o Sundberg ai o Andersson, amende ando Sköndal.

O kher le glatengo sas po Bondegatan ando foro. Me žjavas te dikhav ka Valodja kašte te na bistrel amen o šiavoŕo. Jekh djes lel man ando vudar e gažji kai lelas sama lestar ai phenel mange.

– Jertisar, manuša ame si te mučis la glata.
– Sostar? pušav me darasa.
– Ame dam les te bariol ande jekh familia, phenda mange voi.

Vurta kado djes sas man deš kroni ke sas man gindo te žjav te khelav ando Tallkrogen. Numa akana dem le love pe jekh taxia ai gelem te anav muŕa deia. Muŕo Del če bunto anklisto!

– So sas tumen gindo te čoren muŕe neputos? čipisarda muŕi dei.

Tsoda le vas ande le kičuria ai dikhelas peske kale jakhentsa pe gažji.

– Puter o vudar te anav le šavoŕes!

Me ai muŕi dei dam andre ande jekh soba kai sas pherdo glati.

– Aljoša, savo si o šiavoŕo? pušla ma muŕi dei. Sikav les mange!

Gero Valodja rovelas kana la les opre ande le angali. Vo nas či jekhe beršesko, vo či žjanelas či kon si voi.

Kana avilam palpale ande bar mai čipilas o Valodja. Sa kudala but kale jakha kai dikhenas, lantsuri kai bašonas, bare zlaga ai ŕoči lulodjantsa, o šiavoŕo daralas katar peski mismo dei. Vo sas sikado te dikhel le gažian kai sas le parne ŕoči ai vunitsi jakha.

Ferdi man sas kai prinžarelas, kadia kerdjilem me sar lesko dad makar ke vi me simas glata.

Disease came to the camp. Mum's favourite, Josef, had tuberculosis. The risk of infection forced us to leave one of the youngest children in a children's home. It was Valodja, my brother's little son.

The children's home was situated at Bondegatan on Söder. I used to visit Valodja there so he wouldn't forget about us. One Sunday the matron of the children's home came towards me at the door.
"Excuse me, we're going to move your child," she said.
"What for?" I asked frightened.
"He has been adopted," said the matron curtly.
This very Sunday I had ten crowns with me since I had planned to go dancing in Tallkrogen. Now I had to use that money for a taxi instead to go home and get my mum. God damnit, what a commotion there was!
"Are you planning on stealing my grandson?" Mum shouted putting her hands to her waist and staring with her jet-black eyes at the matron.
Unlock the door right now, I'll go and get the kid."
Mum and I were let into a room with lots of pale, wide-eyed children from the children's home.
"Aljosha, which boy is it?" Mum asked. "Point him out to me!"
Valodja cried when she took him in her arms. Poor kid, he wasn't even a year old and didn't know who she was.
When we came back to the camp in Sköndal Valodja cried even louder. All these dark eyes, necklaces and flowery flounced skirts! That poor wretch was afraid of his own mother. He had got used to quiet nurses with quiet blue eyes and white aprons.
I was the only one he recognised so I became a kind of father to him although I was just a child myself.

DEŠUTRINTO ŠERO

Milai opre ando Švedo

Kana avelas o milai le berš kai sas o marimos lasas amenge kamjonuri vunžile ai žiasas opre ando Švedo. Amare kamjonuri line le amendar ke nas voja te čines benzina ando marimos. Numa le kamjonuri kai lasas vunžile žjanas po gazo.

O Josef kerda amenge neve rama kai ramolas pe lende. "Jekh čači orkesta řomani kai djilabade ando Stockholmo ai vi ando radio", kudo šai ramolas ke ame djilabadam ando radio.

Muře pral djilabenas pe le bazaria ai le gažje avenas te khelen makar ke sas le čino ai vi bokh ando šudro marimos, kamenas te nakhaven peske e vriama. Vi le gažjenge sas trudno vremi ando marimos, buten nas le či xabe.

Opre ando Švedo lavas mantsa le Valodjas ando vurdonořo ai žjavas kai e vazgala te rodav amenge xabe. Me dem po gor ke le dježesa kai avenas le ketani pe lende sas vi vurdona kai sas xabe andre. Kudola vurdona kai sas xabe andre sas ta palal.

Kana o gažjo kai čiravelas o xabe sikavelaspe pa e feliastra lavas angle jekh tigaiutsa ai pušavas te šai del man vareso xabe:

– Me sim jekh čořořo řom, šai des man ai le činořes čeřa xabe!

Atunči lelas o gažjo angle mas tsulo, manřo ai vi kaver djeli ai tsolas mange ande tigaiutsa.

Onivar avenas dježesa anda le tsema kai sas ketani anda Niamtso. Pe lenge gada sas o trošol niamtsisko ai von sas po drom te žjan ando Norvego. Pe le dježesa kai avenas opral sas SS-ketani kai sas dokhade anda marimos. Jekh anda le vurdona sas ramome jekh trošol po vudar.

CHAPTER THIRTEEN

Summers in the Northland

In the summer during the war we rented trucks and went away to the Northland. Our own cars had been confiscated and no private individuals could buy petrol. But you could still hire trucks which ran on gas.

Josef made new posters. 'True Gypsy orchestra, known from Stockholm and the Radio Service' he could print, because by now we had performed on the radio.

My brothers rented dancing floors at all the recreation grounds and the Northlanders came on their bikes. These Northlanders, they knew how to dance even with big worries and an empty stomach. They knew how to get over the darkness of the winter and the war!

It was difficult for the Swedes too during the war. Many people suffered from a shortage of food. In the Northland I used to take Valodja with me in the pram and walk to the railway stations and try to find some food. I had discovered that the trains with passing soldiers had a restaurant carriage. Usually it was one of the last carriages of the trains.

When the chef appeared at the window I held out my pot and pleaded:
"I'm a poor Gypsy, give me and the boy some food!"

Then the chefs cut up some pork and bread and put a bit of this and a bit of that in my pot.

Sometimes there were trains coming from the south with German soldiers. They had swastikas on their uniforms and they were on their way to Norway. The wounded SS soldiers were being transported on the trains coming from the north. One goods wagon on each train had a cross

Kotse si sa mule andre, davas ma gindo me.

Sikavavas muři tigaiutsa lenge ai von tsonas mange andre papiroši ai le Valodjas denas guglimata ai phenenas:

– Ach schönes Kind!

Kudola ketani anda Niamtso sas domoli, terne rakle, nas but mai phure mandar. Či lenge nai drago te mudaren manušen, davas ma me gindo.

painted on the sliding door. That's where the dead are, I thought to myself.

I held out my pot to the German soldiers and they put cigarettes in it. They threw out chocolate for Valodja and said:

"Ach, schönes Kind!"

Those German soldiers, they were ordinary boys, just a year or two older than me. I reckoned they didn't really want to kill people. Not at heart they didn't.

Mum and her sister-in-law. Gypsy women used to always dress in long frilly skirts. Girls were reckoned as adults at 13–14 years old after which it was immoral to show their legs.

Muři dei ai lake šugoritsi. Řomane žjuvlia kanagodi voriavenas pe ande le lungi roči. Le šeiořa djindonas bare kana sas 13–14 beršenge ai antunči sas lažav te sikaves le punře.

DEŠUŠTARTO ŠERO

Škola ande tsera

I vende pale bešasas ande bar ando Sköndal. Numa mai trudno sas amenge te šai trajis. Naštisas mai te trajis sar trajisas pe le purane vremi. Le vremi pařudjile. Le tigei le xarkune či mai žjanas ke akana sas mai but aluminioske ai sastrone.

Muřo dad kamelas te tsol amen le řomen mai te malavas ando tsem. Žjalas ka le bare rai ai mangelas pe lendar:

— Tume kai porončin musai te den amare glaten škoļi te sičon! Den ame škoļi ai khera!

Muřo Del sodi dilimata ašunelas muřo dad katar le gažje kai kerenas pe godjaver.

— Te dasa tumen khera sar keren anda tumaro trajo kai san sikade te phiren, nai tumen kado ande tumaro rat?

— Či san tume le řom sikade ando šil mai but sar le kaver manuš?

— Si tumen le řomen řavda te sičon te djinen tume kai san čirade?

Kadia šai phenenas amenge butivar. Jekh gažjo kai sas anda khangeri kai bušolas Kurt Strömqvist ai jekh doxtoro kai bušolas John Takman, ai vi o prinso, kai porme anklisto amperato o Gustav VI, line love anda peske posoča te šai ažutin amen.

Pala but vriama avili jekh školaritsa ande bar. Voi anda pesa djeli kai trobunas ame te šai sičuvas. Savoře kai kamenas šai lenaspe ande laki škola.

Detradjine avelas jekh suitarka pe bicikleta te sičarel le žjuvlian te suven kritintsi ai te lašaren le glatenge gadořa. Ande lako bufari sas la poxtana ai tsava ande le mai šukar ferbi.

CHAPTER FOURTEEN

The tent school

In the winter we stayed in the camp in Sköndal. But it got harder and harder for us to earn our living. We couldn't survive like we used to any longer. Times had changed. Pots made of aluminium and stainless steel started to replace the copper pots.

Dad tried to fit us Gypsies into the Swedish community, he called on authorities as well as members of the parliament and politicians and pleaded:

"Please, you are in power, our children need education! Give us schools and houses!"

My God, how much stupid talk Dad had to listen to from those Swedish gentlemen with their university degrees.

"If you get houses, what about your wandering blood then?"

"Gypsies you can stand the cold better than other people, can't you?"

"Do you impulsive people really have the patience to learn how to read?"

It could sound like that.

A Salvation Army officer named Kurt Strömqvist, the panel doctor, John Takman, and the crown prince himself, who later became King Gustav Adolf VI, took money out of their own pockets to help us.

Finally, we got a school teacher for our camp. She brought with her desks, pencils and books. Everybody who wanted to could start in her class. Every Wednesday a needlework teacher came on a bike. She was to teach the women how to sew aprons and patch children's clothes. In her suitcase there were wonderfully coloured textiles and yarns.

Our classroom in a tent.

Amari škola ande tsera

— Tu kai san e mai dumolo ai mai gugli, naštiv vi me te suvav tumentsa?

Kača sas jekh phuri žjuvli, kai ande laki klasa šoha nas jekh murš, phenda voi. Numa sar me pušlem la kadia šukares mukla man te zumavav. Me simas kai avavas mai mišto svako tetradji. Mange nas khanči ke prasanas ma muře pral, ferdi te šai suvav.

O djinimos ai o ramomos sas mange čino. Butivar sas mange čino te dav man gindo. Me davas man gindo te čiravav ai te lav sama katar o Valodja. Vo phenelas mange dad, ke me lavas sama lestar ai davas les te xal ai vi davas ma vi gindo ke trobul man love.

The school teacher, Karin Hartman, came from Birkagården in Stockholm.

Karin Hartman bušolas e skolaritsa, voi sas anda Birkagården.

"Please, kind, sweetest Miss, can I please join you in the sewing and needlework", I pleaded.

This teacher was an older lady, she said she'd never had a boy doing needlework. But since I asked her so kindly she let me have a try at it. I became her most hard-working Wednesday pupil and I didn't care about my brothers teasing me, as long as I could crochet and sew the tea cosies and table-cloths.

I thought the reading and the spelling was hard work. I didn't have time to concentrate on it everyday either. I had the cleaning and the cooking to take care of and now I had Valodja too. He called me Dad and I was the one who saw to it that he got food and had clothes to wear. I needed money for that.

Party at Bondegatan. You can see our icons in the background.

Pačiv pe Bondegatan. Ta palpale dičon amare ikoni.

Me lem ma te vuriavav man melales kana žjavas te drabarav. Atunči keravas mai but love te šai žjav ando cine ai te žjav te khelav. Onivar činavas jekh cigara muřе dadeske, ai le Josefoske kai xasalas rat činavas jekhĭ šukar gad.

Jekh djes bešavas avrial e bari khangeri ando purano foro le Valodjasa ando vurdon. Či žjanav sar kerdem vareso le vastentsa ai lenaspe le gažje te den amen love, me gindiv ke mila sas lenge amendar ke anasas čořоře ai melale, muřе papuči sas šinde ai muřе gada sas sane.

Avri ande lumia inke sas marimos, ando Niamtso sas o Hitler baro. Ai le ketani mudarenas muřе narodos ande le kampuri. Naštinas te našen ando Švedo. Kate či lenas andre řomen katar o berš 1914–54.

My niece and I are dancing jitterbug. Little Fred is more interested in the accordion.

Me ai muře praleski šei khelas jitterbug. O činořo Fred mai drago leske e draška.

I started to dress a little more casually when I went fortune-telling. Then I earned more and got enough money for the cinema and dancing. Sometimes I bought a cigar for Dad and I bought a silk shirt for Josef, who was coughing blood.

One day I was standing with Valodja in his pram outside Storkyrkan in Old Town. I don't know how it happened, I made a gesture and reached out my hand and then people passing by came and put money in it. They must have thought that Valodja and I looked foreign and miserable. My shoes were bad and my clothes were thin.

There was a war going on in the outside world. Hitler was in power in Germany and the Nazis where killing my people with gas there. They couldn't flee to Sweden. There was a prohibition of immigration for Gypsies here during the years 1914–54.

Le ivenda sas čoře, merasas šilestar ande amare tseri ai kherořa. O iven ando berš 1944 mekle amen te bešas ande jekh purano kher pe Bondegatan ando Stockholmo. O kher sas kristianongo ai sas phandado katar le raj ke pra purano sas. Numa ame bešlam 17 žjene andre, ferdi te na ašunel khonik ke ame bešas andre.

Kana avilo o milai pale mučisailam palpale ande bar ando Sköndal. Kotse mai arakhadjilo amenge jekh činořo. Vo arakhadjilo vurta o djes kana anklista pača (Fred) ande sa e lumia, paraštune ando majo 1945, ai sar o šiav avilo radoimasa o djes la pačako dam les o anav Fred.

The winters during the war were terrible. We were cold in our tents and barracks. In the winter of 1944 we got to stay in an unfashionable apartment on Bondegatan on Söder in Stockholm. The house was owned by the Salvation Army and the apartment had been condemned by the health service authorities. But we scrubbed it clean, and we got to stay there, seventeen of us, as long as we pretended we didn't exist.

When the spring arrived we moved out to the camp in Sköndal again. Another child of ours was born there. It was on the very day peace was declared, in May 1945, and the boy who came with such happiness got the name Fred [which means peace in Swedish]

DEŠUPANŽTO ŠERO

Jekh rajeski avlin ando Tantolunden

Akana kana o marimos getosailo ankliste le vremi mai laše. Ande Europa pale saste lenpe te lašaren sa so rimosailo ando marimos. Le febriči trobulas le narodo, o Wilhelm la peske buči ka LM Ericsson te tradel kamiono. O Vošo kerelas buči sar dirzari ai muřo dad pale sas les so trobulas les te šai hanol.

Dine ame jekh purani avlin ando Tantolunden paša e Årsta kai či mai bešelas khonik.

Mai anglal sas kudalengi kai kerenas o zaro. Numa ando marimos bešenas ketani andre. Von lenas sama le džežesa kai avenas andre ando Stockholmo.

Akana manas khonik ande avlin. Kado sas te anklel amaro nevo kher

At the manager's villa in Tantolunden.

E avlin ando Tantolunden

CHAPTER FIFTEEN

A fine villa in Tantolunden

Now that the war was finally over times were getting better. Europe was to be rebuilt, the factories needed workers. Wilhelm got a job at L.M. Ericsson as a truck driver, Vosho started working in the scrap business and Dad could find material to do his tinning again.

An old manager's villa at the foot of the Arsta Bridge in Tantolunden became available.

It used to belong to a sugar works but during the war years soldiers had been living there. They had protected the bridge and guarded the fragile railway connection to Stockholm.

Now the residence was abandoned. It was to be our new home and we were to get rooms as big as dance halls. But first every corner of the house needed cleaning up.

My brother's three children on the stairs of the villa at the Årsta Bridge.

Muře trin nepotsi pe skara ande avlin pe Årsta.

ai sas te avel amen sobi bare sar jekh birto khelimasko. Numa akana trobulas te vužiaras o kher ande svako kultso.

Jekh djes kana gelem te anav pai ande dui vedri dikhlem jekh baro soboloko pe skara le khereski. me kerdem sar kana godi, zalisailem. Muřo pral o Josef da man dui trin pelmi te šai vuštav.

– So kerdan? čipilas vo pe mande. Zalisto sar jekh žjuvloři sar kerdjilan tu kadia kovlořo. So gindis ke si ma lon te vuštavav tut?!

Porme čimai phenda khanči. Muřo žjukel o Bobby avilo karing mande vačimasa ai langalas. Mila katar o Bobby. O soboloko dandarda leski pulpa ta o rat šurdiolas! Musai sas ta ingeras les ka e špita te suven les ai de den les jekh suv. Atunči pale zalisailem.

Me xaladem o kher trin djes mai anglal sar te mučis amen andre. Muřo Del, če šukar anklista! Me čidem loludja avrial ai tsodem opre gardini ande le feliestri. Akana sas amen jekh kher. Kana avili muři dei o kher strefialas.

Numa le soboloča sas ande muřo gindo sa so simas činořo.

A fine villa in Tantolunden

One day when I was coming in and carrying a bucket of water in each hand I met a big rat on the stairs of the house. I did what I usually did. I fainted. Had a black-out. My brother, Josef, had to slap me on my cheeks until I woke up:

"What's wrong with you?" he yelled. "Fainting like that, like a woman! Who did you get this silliness from? Do you think I've got smelling salts, huh?"

Then he shut up. My dog, Bobby, came limping, whimpering pitifully. Poor Bobby. The rat had bit him in his leg so that his blood was pouring out. We had to take him to the vet to sew him up and give him an injection against lockjaw. Then I fainted again.

I spent three days cleaning up the house before we moved in. My God, how nice it was! I picked roses from the flower borders and put up net curtains in the windows. We had got ourselves a home. When Mum came it was spotlessly clean.

But the rats, they persecuted me throughout my childhood.

Dad had a carpenter in Vuollerim in Lapland build a new caravan for Mum. She really liked it better there than in the villa. In the wagon she had everything she needed and she could decide everything for herself. It was only in the winter that she moved inside the house.

Muřo dad tsoda jekh kaštari anda Lappland te kerel muřa deiake jekh nevo vurdon. Kotse sas lake mai mišto sar ande avlin. Ando vurdon sas la sa so trobulas la ai kotse purončilas voi. Kana sas iven bešelas pale ande avlin.

Kruglom o kher ando Tanto anklisti jekh antrego bar katar le vurdona ai le tseri. Muře pralenge famili sas bare, o Vošo sas les oxto glati. Muřa deiako pral ai leske glati bešenas vi von amentsa. Ande jekh tsan samas karing 50 žjene ai le vudara sas puterde vi řomenge ai vi gaženge. Muřo dad phenelas:

– Kana godi te avel tut čo ilo ande čo vas.

Onivar ašundjolas sar xanaspe ai čipinas ande peske vurdona ai sobi. Atunči phenasas ame:

– Mai mišto te čipis ai te xastos sar te ankeres e xoli ande tute.

O hanomos ai le řomenge matori meliarenas sa e bar kruglom o kher.

Kana godi sas vi jekh melali glata paša o kher. Numa kana o Ivar Lo Johansson ramosarda pa le řomengi mel ai ke sam jekh narodo kai si amenge drago te phiras atunči dokhada amen zurales. Me lem man te prasav les o Melalo-Johan, kana dikhlem ke sas les jekh melalo gad.

Mum and the famous Swedish writer, Ivar Lo-Johansson

Muri dei ai o Ivar Lo.

A whole camp of caravans and tents grew up around the house in Tanto. My brothers had large families. Vosho had eight children. My uncle and his children were also living with us. Altogether there were almost fifty of us and the doors were open both to Romanies and Swedes. There was hospitality galore.

"You should carry your heart in your hand," Dad used to say.

Sometimes we heard arguing and quarrels and raised voices from wagons and rooms. Then we used to say:

"It's better to shout than to swallow the curse and carry the evil in your stomach."

Because of the tinning and the men's cars it looked untidy around the villa. Sure, there was always a dirty kid around, too but when the author, Ivar Lo-Johansson, wrote about the Gypsies' dirt and wanderlust, then we were hurt. I started calling him Dirty Johan when I saw his soiled shirt collars.

DEŠUŠOVTO ŠERO

O vušimos

Ame le řom kai sam jekh narodo kai phiras šoha nas te das ando gor te trajis te na inkerdamas zorales po vužimos ai amaro zoralo zakono. Ando zakono o řomano si te aves vužo vi andral ai vi avrial. Kudo kai si bi zakonosko ašel rigate katar e kompania.

Muři dei sas kai sičarelas ma sar ame le řom inkeras o vužimos. Ka muři dei sas jekh baro tokato xarkuno kai anda pesa anda Řusia ži ando Tanto. Ande kudo tokato xalavasas amare gada ande jekh lixia (zuralo drab).

CHAPTER SIXTEEN

Cleanliness and purity

We Gypsies probably wouldn't have survived as a nomadic people if we hadn't been so clean and had such strong morals. In our tradition outer and inner cleanliness go together. If you are immoral you are declared unclean.

It was Mum who taught me how we Gypsies should keep everything clean. Mum had a giant copper cauldron which she had carried with her from Russia all the way to Tanto. In that cauldron we boiled our laundry in strong bleach.

It was important to dress neatly in my family. Even when Dad was working he wore a suit and a tie. This is him repairing a copper cauldron.

Ande muŕi familia sas bari buči te aves šukar vuriado. Vi kana kerelas buči muřo dad sas vuriado kurvatasa. Katka lašiarel jekh tigaia.

Anglones tsasas le gada ande trin balaja, ande jekh balaj tsolas muře dadeske ai le šiavenge gada, ai ande jekh balaja tsolas le piškiria le vasunenge ai kai khosasas o mui. Ande trito balaj tsolas le kaver gada, či hamisas le gada ande jekh tsan, numa pařuvelas o pai kana xalavelas le muřsenge gada ai kana xalavelas le žjuvliange gada.

Vi kana xalavenas le vasuri sas le kaver balaja. Muři buči sas te anav pai katar e xaing. Butivar žjavas palpale ai angle te anav pai. Muři buči sas vi te šurav pai pe muře dadeske vas mai anglal sar te xal.

Nas ka svako glata lako tazo te tson pe, numa me kai simas pra raikano kerdem kači ta muři dei činda mange jekh tazo. Kudo tazo nas kon asbal les, me lavas sama lestar sar muře dui jakha.

Kana xalavavas ma lavas ma sama te na dikhel ma khonik ke kudo sas mange lažiav. Kana trobulas te xalavav man vai trobulas te žjav ando veš žjavas čordanes diminiatsi vai ratjako kana či dikhelas khonik.

Ande jekh djes dikhlem jekha anda muře šugoritsa sar xalavelas peske šukar bal. Me šoha ande muřo trajo či dikhlem jekh kasavatar šukar žjuvli. Mai čeřa ai zalivas.

Porme kana arakhlem la Gina dem man gindo so dikhlem ai voi peli mange drago ande muřo ilo.

    First we put the clothes to soak in three different bowls, one bowl for Dad's and the boys clothes and in another bow the washing up cloths and the handkerchiefs. We put our other clothes in the third bowl. We didn't mix clothes just anyhow and we changed the water in the big copper cauldron between the men's and the women's clothes.

The dishes had their own bowl too and there was another for rinsing them.
    It was one of my chores to get water from the well. There were many trips each day. It was also my job to pour water from a ladle over Dad's hands before he ate.
    It was unusual for children to have their own wash-basin but I who was so fussy kept nagging at Mum until she bought me a basin. I used to watch over that possession like an Alsatian. No one could touch my valuable white china!
    I had to be very careful while washing myself so that I didn't show my body in any shameful way. When I had to wash or go out in the woods in the morning and in the evenings I sneaked away so nobody noticed. The men sneaked one way and the women another. It was important that we didn't embarrass each other in the woods or run into each other alone in the dark.
    One day I happened to surprise one of my sisters-in-law while she was washing. She had no blouse on and her hair was hanging loose over the upper part of her body. I had never seen anything more beautiful. I almost fainted.
    Then when I met Gina I was reminded of that sight and that's why I fell so madly in love with her.

DEŠUEFTATO ŠERO

Gina

E Gina sas anda e Dalarna, lako anav sas čačes Lill-Anna. voi sas ansurime jekh raklesa kai vi vo sas anda Dalarna. Vo butivar avelas te phiravel pe ka muřo dad ke von žjanenas pe de sar sas o marimos.

Ande kudola vriemi naštisas te čines mai but sar dui butelči řičia ando šion. Muřo dad nas leske drago o pimos numa univar pelas peske jekh vai dui kana la Ginako gažjo lelas leske te pel.

Jekh riat kana la Ginako gažjo bešelas ai pelas muře dadesa ai muře pralentsa, boldaspe e Gina karing mande ai pušla man:

– Kames te žjas te khelas?

Voi phenelas ke lako trajo sas te khelel. Ame gelamtar ando Tallkrogen te khelas, kotse kana kelasas gindivas ke vuriav, ame dui kerdjilam sar jekh manuš.

Me simas jekh limalo šavořo kam simas 15 beršengo. Me či ačaravas khanči. Ai či muři dei ai muřo dad ai či la Ginako gažjo.

Jekh riat čumida ma e Gina ai me dilajlem! Khonik či čumida ma de sar simas činořo. Mai angle porme da ma jekh žuto strinfi kai sas lake gažeske. Atunči me čindem lake loludja te tsol peske po balkono.

Lasas ame te arakhadjios čordanes, onivar ande le kafanavi vai ando cine, numa mai butivar žjasas te khelas.

Muřo Del sar khelelas e Gina! O khelimos inkerelas amen ande jekh tsan.

O Josef da po gor so kerasas ai phuřisarda ma ka muři dei.

CHAPTER SEVENTEEN

Gina

Gina was a woman from Dalarna and her real name was Lill-Anna. She was married to a fine man from Dalarna who used to come and visit my dad. They used to pass the time together during the war. In those days alcohol was rationed and Dad could only buy two litres of brandy a month. Dad was no drinker but he liked a brandy when Gina's husband offered it. One night while Gina's husband sat talking and drinking with my dad and my brothers, Gina turned to me and asked:

"Will you be my dance partner?"

She told me she loved to dance. We went to the outdoor dance floor at Tallkrogen and we flew around there. We were like one single body joined together. I was only a boy, around fifteen years or so. I didn't understand anything. And neither did Mum or Dad or Gina's husband.

One night Gina gave me a kiss. I was shocked! No one had kissed me since I was a baby. A little later she gave me a pair of socks which weren't worn out and which belonged to her husband. Then I gave her flowers to put on her balcony.

We started seeing each other in secret, sometimes at cafés or cinemas but most of the time at dance-floors. My God, how Gina danced! It was irresistible, the dance brought us together.

Josef discovered us and gossiped to Mum.

– Kames te les tuke jekh řom kai šai avel čo šiav!

– Jo me kamav les, phenda e Gina.

Muřo dad ai muři dei kamenas te lav mange jekh terni žjuvli kai sas anda amaro narodo o řomano. Von sikavenas mange pherdo šukar šeia numa muřo gindo naštinas te pařoven. Me simas sar ando čeri la Ginasa.

Naštiv te phenav ke muřo dad ai muři dei sas xuliariko pe mande, numa von daranas. So avela amare mai činoře šiavesa kai kamel te ansuril pe jekha rakliasa kai si ansurime?

Sa vurtosaila amenge pala jekh drama frantsuzisko kai me ai Gina dikhlam ando cine po Hornsgatan jekh savato.

– Mangav ma tumendar, žjan ai dikhen la vi tume, phendem muře dadeske ai deiake. Me pučinav tumenge le mai laše tsana ferdi te žjana te dikhen la!

E drama sikavelas sar jekh terni rakli sas te ansurilpe jekhe phure rajesa kai sas barvalo. Jekh drabarni da la raklia jekh butela kai sas andre jekh drab kamimasko. Kudo trobulas te piel kaste řivdil te trajil le grofosa. Numa so anklista, kai o grofo sas jekh nanito jagalo kai kerelas leske buči. Vo la o drab le kamimasko ai da les ka le grofosko neputo.

Akana o nepuro dilailo anda e rakli, numa o grofo o barvalo či kamla te mukel la raklia le neputoske. Kadia le dui terne ando nekezimos line ai mule ande jekh tsan. Ke vi e rakli kamelas le neputos.

Kana muřo dad ai muři dei avile khere phende mange:

– Lela Aljoša! Namai de tu gindo pe le niamuri. Traji čo trajo sar alosardan ča žjuvliasa! Te svuntsol tumen o Del.

La Ginake šiave vuže bare sas ai mučisaile kheral, ai lako gažjo ašilo te mukenpe ai te vulavel le mubluri.

"You can't have a husband who's young enough to be your son!" Mum said to Gina.

"Yes, I love him." answered Gina.

Of course, Mum and Dad wanted me to marry a young, untouched woman from our own people. They suggested one beauty after the other to me. But I was firm. I had been enchanted by Gina.

You couldn't say Mum and Dad were angry, they were worried. What would happen to their youngest son who had fallen in love with a married Swedish woman?

Thanks to a French film it all worked out in the end. Gina and I had seen it at Sandrews cinema at Hornsgatan one Saturday night.

Please go and see that film," I said to Mum and Dad. "I'll buy you tickets to the stalls if only you'll go and see it!"

The film was about a poor young woman who was to be married to an older rich nobleman. The girl had been given a bottle with love potion from a sorceress. She was to drink it to be able to cope with the old earl. But it turned out so bad that the nobleman's servant, a cunning dwarf, gave the love potion to the count's young nephew instead!

The dwarf laughed, but the cinema audience screamed with fright. Of course, the count didn't want to give up his beautiful young bride and this brought about the ruin of the young romantic lovers. Their hearts broke and they died together.

When Mum and Dad came home from the cinema they said:

"Take the woman, Alyosha. Never mind your family. Live happily with the one you have chosen! May God bless you."

Gina's own two children had already grown up and moved away from home and her husband agreed to divorce her if he got to keep half of the furniture.

DEŠUOXTOTO ŠERO

Abiav

Kana pherdjilem muře beršengo ansurisailam ande khangeri kai bušolas Allhelgonakyrkan. Muřo dad či mai trajilas atunči. Muři dei kerda mange jekh baro abiav makar ke me ansurisailem jekha rakliasa kai sas anda Dalarna.

Kana avilam ande khangeri phirenas dui glati angla amende o Valodja ai e Madoka, (voi sas šukar sar jekh papuša).

Dui trin djes gela muřa deiake ai muře šugoritsenge te lašaren o xabe le abiavesko. O xabe trobulas te aresel šele žjenenge. Pe skafidi sas maše, kolompiria, boršo, gulasch, piroški, biš kainja, dui bare šunkoria, tutkaia, bare masa ai sarmi.

O pekarniaš o Gunnar kai sas les pekarnia kai muřo pral butivar hanolas leske tigei, anda dui bare pirožni. Muři dei muli asaimastar lestar.

– Muřo Del! Kudo aresel ferdi le glatenge. phen če manušenge te peken mai but pirožni!

Pala mismeri anda o Gunnar mai efta pirožni, Ai ande matora sas pherdo kaver guglimata. Ai ratjako či ašila khanči.

Muře pral ande bare palia kai khelel o manuš pe lende, katar e feria, ai ratjako ašundiolas e djili le abiaveski pe sa o Tanto. Le manuš kai bešenas paša amende sas gažje ai von bariarenas loludja. Von avile ka abiav ai ande amenge šukar loludja ai amenge sas drago.

– Aven xan ai pen vi tume amentsa, radoisame ande jekh tsan! So mai but manuš mai but radoimos.

Ame mardam kai le gazeturia te aven te len patretsi pe amende ai te ramon pa o abiav. Mamo, mamo so mačile le gazetaria! Khonik či pila kadia but sar lende.

CHAPTER EIGHTEEN

Marriage

We married in All Saints Church when I became of age. By then Father was dead and Mother arranged a big wedding for me, even though I was marrying a Gorgio woman. We had two 'bridesmaids', Valodja and Madoka – who looked as sweet as a doll.

Mother and my sisters-in-law had been cooking food for many days before the wedding banquet. There had to be enough for a hundred guests. There was herring, potatoes, salmon and eel, beetroot soup and goulash, dumplings, twenty cooked chickens, two giant hams, turkey, roast veal and stuffed cabbage.

Gunnar the baker, who my brother Vosho used to do tinning for, came with two large cream cakes in the morning. Mum laughed at him, "My God. That'll be just enough for the children. Tell your people to bake some more."

In the afternoon Gunnar came with seven more cakes from his bakery and his car was full of boxes with freshly baked Danish pastries and small cakes.

Everything was fine.

My brothers had borrowed a dance floor from a fair and in the evening wedding music could be heard over the whole of Tanto. Our nearest neighbours were Swedes who had holiday cabins there and they came by with freshly picked bouquets of flowers and
we made them welcome.

"Dearest friends, eat and drink and share our joy. The more guests the more good luck."

We had phoned the newspapers so they could come and take photos and write about the wedding. Oh dear, how drunk the journalists got. No one

Či muře ai či la Ginake niamuri nas lenge vušoro ke ame ansurisailam. La Ginaki dei kadia lažaili ta geli kai lavka kai sas paša lende ando Dalarna ai činda sa le gazeturia kai ramonas pa amaro abiav. Porme dale jag ando bov. Vi le patretsi le abiaveske kai tradam lake la ai phabarda le.

Gina got Mum's silver belt as a wedding present.

Muři dei da la Gina c kuštik c ruponi sar pudarka abiaveski.

drank as much as the newspaper men.

Both Gina's and my family had trouble accepting that we were going to get married. Gina's mother was so ashamed that she went to the kiosk in Dalarna and bought up all the papers that wrote about our wedding. Then she burnt them all in the oven. She also burnt the wedding photos we had sent. She had nothing against Gypsies. She was just an ordinary countrywoman who wanted a farmer as a son-in-law, a strong man that could take over the farm when she herself got old.

Nor did she want a divorced daughter and a weakly Gypsy who was

Nas ke voi či kamelas le řomen. Voi sas jekh žjuvli bučarni ai voi kamelas jekh žjamutro kai vi vo sas pavero sar late, jekh zuralo manuš kai šai kerel lake buči kana voi phuriola.

Sa či kamelas voi jekh phuvli šei ai jekh kuvlo žjamutro kai daralas katar o tuniariko ai katar le soboloča. Ai vi šai avilosas lako neputo!

Muři dei jertisardia amen po djes le abiavesko.

– Če bori lem mange phenda voi. Či pařodemas la či pe jekh řomani šei!

O kaver djes gelamtar ando Saltsjöbaden te phiravas ame

afraid of the dark and rats. And apart from that he could have been her grandson.

Mum forgave us before the wedding.

"What a daughter-in-law I've got," she said. "I wouldn't change her for a Gypsy girl, may the Devil take me."

The next day we set off for Saltsjöbaden for our honeymoon.

DEŠUENJATO ŠERO

Buči, kher ai glati

E Gina la peske buči ka Eriksdalsbadet (kotse sas kai naiolas pe). Me lem mange buči ka jekh fabrika kai kerenas lempi. Kana gelem te mangav e buči dikhelas e raji la fabrikaki pe mande.
 – Me či kamav romen ande muri fabrika, phenda voi.
 Me simas melaxno ai nas man laše rama katar e škola, nas ma či vurta rama kai arakhadjilem.
 – Mangav man tutar rajio, le man po zumaimos jekh kurko. Me sim jekh lašio manuš.
 E buči sas te bešes ka jekh mašinka ai te tsos rama pe lempi kai tsolaspe pe jolka. E buči sas tristo numa mange sas drago muře vurtača kai e buči. Dine ma e buči bi te zumaven man. Ai kotse kerdem buči but berš.
 Mai anglal sar te lav la Gina phendem lake:
 – Gina, me si te avav tusa čačo ande sostegodi, ma kamav te žjanes ke kana avela o milai, atunči me naštiv te bešav maškar štar ziduria. Me musai te avav avri te ačarav e barval.
 Vi e Gina sas sar mande. Lake sas drago o kham ai le loludja. Po milai lelas ma pesa ka pesko kheroŕo ando Dalarna, ai me lavas la mantsa kotse kai djilabenas muře pral. Tsodam amari tsera paša lenge vurdona ai e Gina lelas pe te sičol te del duma řomanes ai vi te drabarel.
 Trajisas sar řom kana sas o milai ai sar gaže kana avasas khere.
 O Valodja sas amentsa kači ta akana musai sas te phenav leske:
 – Muŕo drago Valodja, me či sim čo dad. Akana san baro ai musai tuke te bešes ka čo čačo dad ai dei.
 Numa vi adjes phenel mange o Valodja dada.

CHAPTER NINETEEN

Work, a flat – and children

Gina got a job on the cash desk at Eriksdal Baths. I worked in the Osram electric light bulb factory. When I went looking for that work, the head of the section looked doubtfully at me.

"I don't want any Gypsies here," she said.

I was dark of course and I had neither a school leaving certificate nor a real birth certificate.

"Take me on trial for a week, madam," I begged. "I am an honest man."

The job consisted of sitting by a machine and filling boxes for Christmas lights. It was a little monotonous but I got on well with my co-workers and in the end I stayed at that factory for many years.

Before I married Gina I said to her,

"Gina, I will be faithful to you in everything but you need to know that when summer comes, then I can't live between four walls. Then I have to get out and breathe fresh air." Gina, she was the same. She liked the sun and flowers like me. In our holidays she took me to her chalet in Dalarna and I took her to the parks there where my brothers hired dance floors and played. We stayed in a tent next to their caravans and Gina learnt both to tell fortunes and to speak Romani.

Sv. Fabriks avd. 32 40 års Jub. Mosebacke 8.3.1958

The factory trade union branch celebrates its fortieth anniversary in Mosebacke

O fabrikako sindikato kerel pačiv ando Mosebacke

Kana anzarde o Bredäng dine ame khera kotse. Muči-sailam andre numa inke nas vurta gata le khera. Soba soimaski ai salono, kuxnia ai vi kai šudes o gunoj. Vi pai sas ame ando kranto. Kado sas amenge sar o řaio! Putravas o kranto ai avelas o tato pai sar kai phirel ando Jordan.

– Nais tuke dei devleski! čipivas me.

Porme kači nailem ta musai sas e Gina te makhelma ande kremi ke muři morči šučili.

Kana arakhadjilo o Mario e Gina bešelas lesa mai but khere. Voi sas šukar sar jekh amperatiasa ai vi o činořo sas šukar sar jekh činořo amperatutso!

Lavas pe leste vunitsi gada ai parne papuči. O narodo boldenas pe pala leste ai pušenas sar bušol.

– Mario.

Ame kamasas les.

Kana o Mario lape ande škola vi me lem man te kerav buči. Či kamavas te lažialpe o šiavořo kana kamlosas te ažutiv les la školasa ai me či žianavas te djinav. Me lem man ande jekh škola ando Årsta. Linepe te

We lived a Gypsy life in the holidays and a Swedish life for the rest of the year.

Valodja stayed with us till he was grown up enough so I could say to him:

"Dear Valodja, I'm not your father. Now you're old enough to live with your real parents."

But even today Valodja calls me Dada which means Father in our language.

When Bredäng was built we got a flat there. We moved in even though it wasn't ready. Bedroom and sitting room and kitchen. Lift. Rubbish chute. Running water. What paradise. I twisted the taps and the hot water spurted out like a waterfall on the River Jordan.

"Thank you Holy Mother of God," I shouted.

Afterwards I had a bubble bath everyday until my body got so dry that Gina had to rub in Nivea cream all over me.

After our son, Mario, was born Gina became a housewife. She was as beautiful as a queen and as for the boy, he was as sweet as a little prince. I dressed him in a dark blue sailor suit and white shoes. People used to turn round in the street and ask what he was called.

"Mario."

We loved him.

Mario

When Mario started school I began to study, too. I didn't want the boy to be ashamed when he learnt that his father couldn't read his lessons with him. I started in Årsta Folk High School. They started a course for Gypsies who were illiterate and I there got a career adviser called Janne Kage.

I loved to stand on the hill near Gina's chalet with Mario in my arms. From there we could see the mountains and four towns.

Mišto sas mange kana bešavas opre kai la Ginako kher le Mariosa ande le vas. Kotsar opral šai dikhasas le plajina ai štar gavoŕa.

sičaren ŕomen kai či žjanen te djinen. Amaro školari bušolas Janne Kåge.

– Sostar kames te keres buči, Nisse? pušla kado manuš.

Če pušimos! Me kai kerdem buči de sar lem man te phirav, me kai simas khelitori, kai kerdem buči pe feria, kai tradem kamiono, kai makhavas manŕe, kai kerdem buči ande fabrika, kai servivas ande kafanava. Sostar kamav te kerav buči? Pe kado pušimos musai sas te dav man gindo.

– Me kamlemas te ažutiv kudo len kai si nasvale. Numa kudo či pačav ke žjal pe? Či pačav ke maladjolpe te kerel jekh ŕom buči ka jekh špita?

Ai čačes, but sas kai phenenas ke či maladjolpe, vi maškar muŕe manuš ai vi maškar le gažje. Maškar muŕo narodo naštilaspe te kerel jekh ŕom buči nasvalentsa. Ame le ŕom phenas ke jekh ŕom naštil te azbal le gada la žjuvliake. Ai me kai ažutivas bute žjuvlian kai avenas ande špita kerdem jekh djela kai či maladjolas ando zakono o ŕomano. Kadia ašilem rigate katar muŕi familia.

"What work do you want to do, Nils?", the man asked me.

What a question. Me, who had worked since I could walk. Me, who had been a dancer, bass player, fairground worker, berry picker, sandwich maker, waiter, messenger boy, driver, factory worker, what work did I want to do? That question needed some time to think.

"I'd like to help sick people," I risked answering after a while. Even though I knew that wouldn't work. It's not going to be right for a Gypsy to work in caring for the sick.

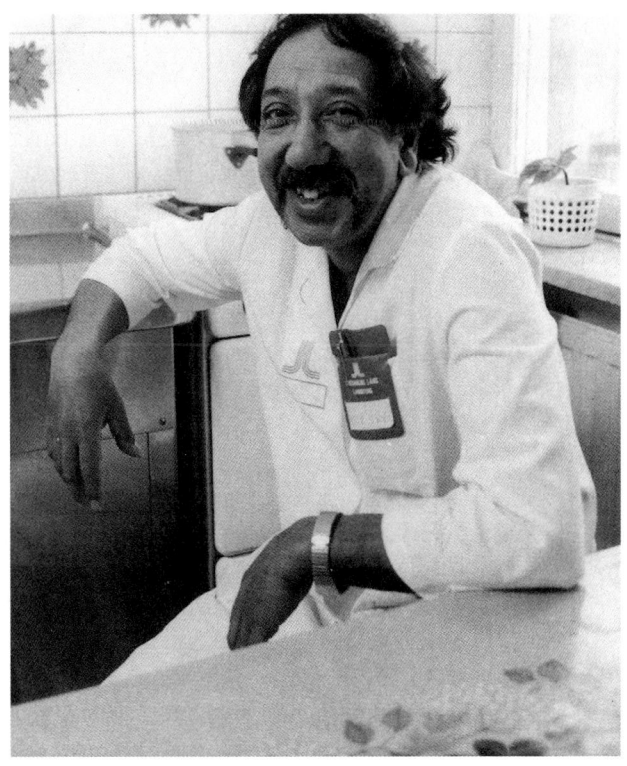

I liked my work at St Göran's Hospital. The photo was taken around 1970.

Mange sas drago muři buči ka e špita S:t Goran. O patreto si anda berš 1970

And there were many who thought it wasn't right, both my own people and the Swedes. As far as my people were concerned it was unthinkable that a man would tend the sick. We say that a Gypsy man can't, in any circumstances, undress a woman. When I used to lift up patients' blankets, pull up their night-clothes to put a pot there or dress a wound, I was doing something immoral according to our code. I was classed as unclean by my own relatives.

Či ažutilas ke mande sas parni raxami ai manuši pe le vas ai ke xalavavas le vas jekh šelvar o djes. me ašilem rigate katar le řom. Či mai akharenas ma khonik pe jekh kafa. Či kamenas te azbav lenge vasuri.
Le gažje či kamenas le řomen anda kaver djeli. Von gindinas ke ame le řom ferdi čoras. Oni gindinas vi ke čoras glaten katar le gažje. Sar te na avilosas ame dosta glati amen le řomen.

Bax sas ke e Gina sas paša mande. Ame ačarasas jekh avreske. Ame vuže nakhlam opral pa o zakono o řomano. Kerdam so nas slobodo.
E Gina spidelas ma te žjav ande škola, ai phurme lem muřo diplomo kai e S:t Görans gymnasium ke kerdem muři škola vurta.
Dine man buči ka e špita kai bušol S:t Görans po Kungsholmen. Sa kudo djes kai avilem andre ande špita ačardem ke kado sas muřo tsan. Me kerdem buči 25 berš kotse ai drago sas mange svako djes kai žjavas ka muři buči. Getosardem e buči kana phurilem ai dine man jekh časo sumnakono.
Me či phendem khanikaske ke me simas řom, numa sar simas melaxno phenavas ke me sim bastuxo anda Řusia kai bešlem ando Dalarna.
Muře niamuri jertisarde man pala but berš. But anda lende kerdjile kristianuri (pentekostaluri). Von djinenas e biblia ai ande lenge jakha či mai simas marime. Akana simas o lašio samaritano.
Sostar sas mange mišto le nasvalentsa? Ke me anklavas lentsa amigo. Bute nasvalen serav, numa jekha či bistrav, e Margit. La sas nasvalimos ande le kokala (leukemi), le draba či lenas e dokh pa late. Lake kokala sas khuvle sar e vojaga.
– Tristo san Margit? pušelas la o baro doxtoro. žia ka Nils-Erik ai phen leske te khelel tusa.
Atunči tsavas rigate sa so kerava ai khelavas me ai e Margit ži kana sas lake mišto.
– Des ma či vorba ke avesa mantsa kana avela e vriama te merav? pušla ma e Margit. Me dem la muři vorba.
Kudo milai gelemtar me ande Polska. Me phendem ka e špita kai sim ai jekh riat marde mange katar e špita.
– Nils-Erik, musai te aves khere, e Margit nai lake mišto.
Me čindem lake jekh papuša anda e Polska ai tsodem ma ande matura. Pala dui djes simas khere ando Stockholmo. E Margit sas khuvli numa ažukerda pe mande.

It didn't matter that I wore a white uniform and rubber gloves and that I washed my hands a hundred times a day. I was excluded from the Gypsy community. I was no longer invited to drink coffee. I couldn't touch another Gypsy's cups.

Swedes were against Gypsies in another way. They thought that all Gypsies stole, like ravens. Some would even say that Gypsies stole Swedish children. As if we haven't enough with our own Gypsy children.

It was lucky I had Gina to talk to. We understood each other, we had both broken with the laws of our communities, we had both done what was forbidden.

Gina encouraged me to carry on with my education and when I took my care worker's examination at St Göran's Grammar School I got a scholarship for my good results.

I got a job at St Göran's Hospital in Kungsholmen. As soon as I came into the wards I realised I had chosen right. I stayed there for twenty-five years and enjoyed every working day. I didn't stop until I reache pensionable age and got a gold watch.

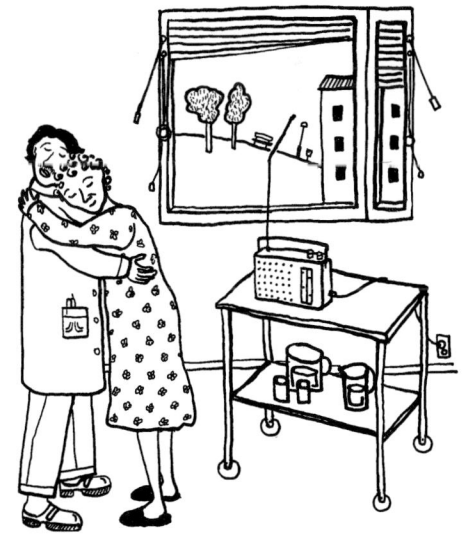

I didn't tell anyone I was a Gypsy. I explained my dark complexion by saying I was an adopted Russian child from Dalarna. My relatives forgave me as the years passed. Many of them had been converted in the Pentecostal Church. They read the Bible and stopped seeing me as someone unclean. Instead, I was the Good Samaritan.

The fact that I felt so satisfied in the ward for long-term sick was because there we became friends with the patients. I

My friends, the mounted police at Kivik market 1980.

Muře vurtača, le raibare po bazari ando Kivik ando berš 1980.

– Akana avilem, phendem lake me ai lem lako vas.
– Ašunes ma Margit?
Atunči la voi ai asaja pe mande. Porme či mai vuštili.
Me dikhlem bute manušen te meren ta me či mai darav katar o merimos. Akana vi me sim phuro. Me či mai ašunav vurta ai muře jakha rimusaile. Naštiv či te suvav mai.

E Gina či mai trajil. Me lem sama latar ži kudo djes kana muli. Sa muře pral mule. Muřo drago šiav mulo.

Me dav man gindo pe muřo trajo. Muřo dad ai muři dei dine man jekh lašio trajo, me ai Gina sas ame lašio trajo, ka muři buči sas mange mišto.

remember many sick people, but especially Margit. She had leukaemia, the medicines couldn't take away the pain. Her body was as brittle as glass.

"Are you miserable, Margit," the tutor would say. "Go to Nils-Erik and ask him to dance with you."

Then I put my work aside and put the radio on. Then Margit and I would dance in the dining room until she felt comforted.

"You promise to be with me when I die," said Margit, "and you'll lay me out afterwards so I look fine."

I promised.

That summer I went on my leave to Poland. I had let them know where I was and one evening I was rung from the hospital.

"Nils-Erik, you must come. Margit is poorly."

I bought a Polish doll for her and got into the car. A few days later I was back in Stockholm. Margit was weak but she had waited.

"Well, here I am," I said, and sat on the side of the bed. I took her hand,

"Can you hear me, little Margit?"

She smiled at me. Then she lost consciousness.

I have seen so many die and am no longer afraid of death. Now I am old myself. I don't hear very well and my eyes are weak. I can hardly sew any more.

Gina is dead. I looked after her at the end. All my brothers are dead. My beloved son Mario is dead.

I think back about my life. My parents gave me a good upbringing, my marriage was a happy one, I enjoyed working in the hospital. I still have relatives and friends alive and one grandchild.

Now I am not afraid to say who I am and where I come from. I have lived in the same flat in Bredäng for thirty years now and I don't have any desire to travel. Here in Bredäng I don't have to be ashamed amongst the Swedes. I have earned my pension.

I buy in the shops and no one keeps an eye on me or thinks that I am going to steal something. I borrow talking books from the library, I go to church, I join in weaving in the pensioners' club. I chat with my neighbours and I give the alcoholics a coin when I pass by them as they sit and freeze on the park bench.

The only thing valuable I own is my mother's silver belt. I had to sell

Si ma niamori ai amiguri ai vi jekh neputo kai inke trajil.

Akana tromav te phenav kon sim ai katar avav. Me bešlem ande jekh kher 30 berš akana, ai te phirav sar mai anglal manai mange po ilo. Katse ando Bredäng či trobul te lažiav maškar le gažje. Ke me kerdem muřo trajo vurta.

Me činav ande le levči bi te lelpe khonik pala mande ke gindin ke čorav. Me lav mange vunžile kniški ka e biblioteka, dav duma le gažientsa kai bešen paša mande, dav univar lovoře ka le mačarne kai bešen po drom ando šil.

E mai šukar djela so ašila man si e kuštik e ruponi muřa deiaki. Le diamantsi kai sas andre musai sas te lav le avri ai te bičinav le ke o Mario xalas but love kana sas terno.

Kudo djes kana me či mai avava si te dav e kuštik ka muři ortodokso khangeri te tson la ande jekh vojaga paša le ikoni.

Numa mai anglal si te žjav ando Kivik po basari. Kotse kai khelavas mange de tsinořo ai drabaravas, khelavas ai vi pilem ande kadala 70 berš! Si te žiav ai lav mange jekh skafidi maškar le kaver kai bičinen po basari ai si te čipiv:

– Ašunen savoře! Na inkeren kadia zurales ande tumare bufaria. Me sim jekh lašio manuš kai ramosardem jekh kniška pa muřo trajo. Aven ai činen e kniška pa o šiav le birevosko pe le řom!

the diamond that was in the middle of the buckle when Mario was young and cost a lot of money. Some time when I am no longer here the belt will be given to my orthodox church and sit there brightly in a glass case among the icons.

But before then I will go to Kivik market where I have played games and told fortunes and danced and drunk for nearly seventy years. There I will rent a stall among all the merry-go-rounds, jugglers and sellers of baubles and shout:

"Look here, good people. Don't hold your wallets so tightly. I am an honest man who is now a writer. Come and buy a book from the Gypsy King's son!"

PART TWO
Johan Taikon's Tales

Introduction

Johan, Alyosha's father, was well known as a story teller not only among the Gypsies but also to many Swedes. He recounted many stories in Swedish to Carl Herman Tillhagen who edited them and published them in the popular book *Taikon berättar* (Stockholm 1946), while Erik Ljungberg published several in the original Romani. The following stories have been taken (and adapted with permission) from Eric Ljungberg's joint volume with Olof Gjerdman *The Language of the Swedish Coppersmith Johan Dimitri Taikon.* (Uppsala 1963).

Erik Ljungberg with Johan Taikon

O Erik ai o Johan

TALE ONE

The magic goldfish

I'll tell you a story, boys and men. May it be for our good health! It was like this and yet it wasn't like this but if it hadn't happened it wouldn't have been told. Candle-wax they ate, candle-wax they drank, that was what they lived on, our Gypsies.

There was an old man and old woman. The old man fished, and the old women spun. He goes out to sea, the old man, and fishes. As he went out to fish … after a while he threw his net into the water, into the sea, and caught nothing, he only fetched up seaweed.

Then he shakes out his net again for the second time; and after that he takes his net up again; there's still nothing. There was nothing this time either. Well, what's this?

Then he says: "For thirty-three years I've been fishing here and not once before now did I not even catch one fish. What strange thing is going on here?"

Well he gets his net ready again, for the third time he prepares it and for the third time he throws it out. See, he caught a fish. It wasn't bad, it was made of gold, and could speak the Romani language, like us.

Well, the little fish says to him … to the old man, this. "Old man, put me back in the sea! If you make soup out of me there won't be much of it! There won't be much, if you cook me."

"Aha, well!"

"But I'll give you as much as you want, all you can think of."

"Good," says the old man. "But how am I to catch you again and how… how am I to know that you are telling me the truth?"

"Well, just listen, old man! Put me back in the sea!"

The old man then lets him go. He goes merrily home to the old woman, even whistling on his way.

"Hey, old woman, I caught a fish today! It wasn't bad, it was golden, and could speak Romani just like us."

"What are you saying, old man?"

"Yes, indeed, it could and then… It said, it would give us whatever we can think of."

"God! But you wretched, unsalted, ugly old man, didn't you have the sense to beg of him at least a new trough? You can see that our tub is cracked here!"

"Oh, old woman, don't nag me, don't scream! Be quiet, and I'll go to the sea shore and call the fish."

The old man went to the seashore. All well and good, fine, he calls the little fish to come to him.

"What do you want, old man?"

"Well, the old woman nags me, she gives me no peace, and she wants a new trough."

"Go back home, old man, that will be all right too."

The old man goes back home, he sees a new trough in front of the old woman.

"Well, old woman, I told you so!"

A day or two passed, the sunset came. Well, as the sun was setting, oh, how the old woman began to nag the old man.

"Why are you scolding me, old woman?"

"Why shouldn't I scold you? We have lived for thirty-three years in this mud hut and you couldn't even ask for a new house for us."

"Very well! Shut up, old woman, don't nag me!"

The old man goes off to the shore again and calls the little fish.

"Well, little fish, listen to me! My old wife nags me, gives me no peace, by day and by night she screams away!"

"But what does she want, old man?"

"The old woman wants a new house!"

"All right, old man, go home and rest, that will also be done."

The old man turned back, towards the home, walked through the forest and jumped over the fence, when he saw that not even a trace of the mud hut is left. What does he see before him but a beautiful new house, its roof was tiled and it even has a veranda in front of it.

He saw the old woman; the old woman is sitting down, she has no longer got the plank she used to sit on, but look what she has: a real spinning-wheel which goes round, round it goes, and works, there's flax and thread.

The old man went in.

"Well, old woman, what do you say now?"

"Shut up, old man, are you going to babble on, or I'll sew up your mouth at once."

The old man doesn't talk. The old man went in and lies down on his back and rests. He lay there for one week, he lay for two, and he even lay for three.

The old woman was bored.

"What do you want old woman?"

The woman began to nag the old man again.

"But, old woman, give me some peace, don't shout at me. Why are you scolding me? What do you want?"

"Listen now, I want... I don't want to be a peasant's wife any longer, I want to be a lady of rank, and drink wine and eat nice cakes."

"All right! Keep quiet, you old woman, stop screaming! Don't make a fuss! I'll go and ask the fish."

He went down to the sea; he goes out there and calls the little fish. The little fish comes to him.

"What do you wish for now, old man?"

"Well, my boy, my good fellow, the old woman scolds me and won't give me any peace. She wants to be a noble woman. And she doesn't want to be a peasant's wife."

"Doesn't she want that? Well, go home again, old man, that shall be done, too."

The old man wends his way home.

What does he see: the old woman! She is sitting inside the house, and she has her servants who wait upon her, and she is drinking wine and eating cakes.

"Now, old woman, you are well off."

"Be off with you, old man, or I'll call for my servants to kill you!"

Well, she sat there for one month, she sat for two, yes, she sat even for three. In the third month she calls the old man in again and says to him:

"Old man, listen, this is what you are to do: go down to the water's edge and tell the little fish that I don't want to be just a lady of rank any more, now I want to be Empress."

"But no, old woman… don't be crazy… for he won't give you that!"

"You must go!"

Well then, the old man sets off to the seashore and he says to the fish, asks the fish, "The old woman is now asking to become… she doesn't want to be a noblewoman anymore but wants to be Empress… and she wants you to be her servant. Whatever she tells you, you are to do!"

"Go back home, old man, that too shall be done."

So the old man goes back again, and what does he see before his eyes! The old woman is still sitting … she is sitting in front of a mud hut and also the cracked tub is there, and she sits and spins her flax, once again on the stool she had.

That's my story, there's no more to it.

TALE TWO

The Gypsy who made his confession

I'll tell you a story, Erik! Well, it was like this and yet it wasn't like this but if it hadn't happened it wouldn't have been told, my Gypsy friend. It doesn't matter that you are a Swede, in spite of that we can speak to each other because you know the Gypsy language just as well as I do.

Well, one Sunday a Gypsy got the idea of going to church. He hears the church bells ringing. "Ah! I will go and pray to the dear holy God!"

First he passed the priest's house. What should he do, or not do. He steals … he begins to search the priest's house. What does he find? Nothing. He searched here and there. Well, what does he find? He looks in the oven. "Bless my mother, he has got roast pig! Wait now, I'll fool him." He takes the pig out and tucks it into his trousers. Then he goes a little further into the room and takes the cap from in front of the icons. Then he comes to the priest.

"Good day to you, Father!'

"Good day to you, Gypsy! What do you want?"

"Indeed Father, it would be good if you could forgive me my sins!"

"Very well, we will do so, my good man. That's why I am a clergyman. I must do that"

He walks on … "Well, my boy, tell me, what sins have you committed?"

"Yes, Father, I have committed sins. I drove the pig away from the potatoes, that I did."

"And what other sins have you committed"

"Oh, my God, Father, I took a cap away from in front of the holy images."

"My boy, those were no sins. The first thing you did, that was a kindness to whoever's potatoes they were. That was well done. And then, that you took a cap away from in front the holy images, that wasn't bad either. That was well done too."

"Well, thank you, Father"

In the meantime while he was making his confession, he took the priest's watch and his snuffbox. The priest goes off and mass is being said in church.

What should he do or not do? The priest points to his nose for the Gypsy, meaning that he shall give him back his snuffbox. What does the Gypsy do?

"Be quiet, Father. May God take away his tongue!" he says.

Well, the priest calms down. He calmed himself again. Then after a while he sees... he begins to think of the time. He feels in his pocket, sees that the watch is not there. The Gypsy stole it from him. Again he does the same, looks at the Gypsy, and makes signs, as if he is looking at his watch, and the Gypsy says, "Father... may God take away his tongue if he says anything."

That's very well, he took the Eucharist... mass is over... the Gypsy goes his way, he too goes home. When he went home, the priest also went home; he comes in cheerfully and happily and says to his wife: "You, take out the pig, the roast pig out of the oven, and the potatoes as well!"

The parson's wife quickly goes to the stove to take out the pig and the potatoes. "Look. Father, nothing is left but the potatoes."

"Never mind, wife, say nothing. Go and look in the parlour, is my cap there?"

The priest's wife goes in and looks. "Your cap is not there"

"Very good, wife, don't say anything!"

And that was my story, there is no more to it, and I have no more to tell you. I leave you with God till another time.

TALE THREE

The cut corn that raised itself

Well, I'll tell you a story again, Erik. It was like this and yet it wasn't like this
but if it hadn't happened it wouldn't have been told.

One day, Gypsies, women, girls were walking on the road singing and dancing. They see a big manor house.
"Listen, men and boys, we'll go there and work!"
And, they went off. One of the Gypsies who knew how to talk, he was, as the Gorgios say, our chief. So the chief went up to the manor.
"Good morning sir, count, king!"
"Listen Gypsy, I am no count, nor am I king, I am a clergyman"
"Oh, so much the better, may God grant you a long life, Father! We are Gypsies, Father, and all our daughters and our wives and children are with us. Can you give us some work to do."
"Work? Yes... but what can you do, you Gypsies?"
"We? We can do everything, Father."
"But can you reap?"
"Yes, of course we can, why shouldn't we know how to do that?"
"Very well then. But now listen, Gypsies! Go ahead and reap the corn! How long do you reckon it will take you to reap so and so much ground, so and so many hectares?"
"That much, Father, we'll do in three days, that we will, both reap it and bind it!"
"Fine!"
"But Father, then you must be so kind as to give us food for three days."

"Yes, of course... I must give you food, good people. Of course I must, you cannot die of hunger."

The priest gives them food for three days. They went to where the grain was. Well, the priest doesn't come down to them. One of them says: "Listen! Eat and drink and sing and don't fear anything."

Three days passed like that. One of the Gypsies says: "Wait! I'll just try and see what it's like to reap." He sets himself to mow a little piece of the field. Well, when he had mown that little piece, he just heaps the corn towards the edge of the furrow.

Those Gypsies, for three days and three nights they ate and drank, and on the fourth day the food was finished. Well, they had nothing more to eat or drink. They go up to the priest, they got themselves ready to leave.

"Good morning, Father!"

"God brings you here Gypsies! Well, how was it?"

"Father, the work is finished. We reaped and bound the corn. Will you please be so kind and pay us!"

"No, good people, I must see it first!"

"Oh, but don't you believe us, Father, that we have done it, we mowed and gleaned and bound the sheaves."

"No, good people, I must see it first!"

"All right, Father, just listen to this!"

The Gypsy kneels and prays to the dear holy God, this is how he prays: "May God make the corn just as it was before!"

Well, he goes off. All the Gypsies go. They ate and drank for three days and then they went on their way. So the priest waited another day or two, then he goes to see his field. Well, when he came to the field, the priest scratches his head.

Well, the dear holy God listened to their prayer and the corn rose again! But look at this one sinner, where he mowed, the corn was not raised again!

That was my story; there is no more to it. Thank you, my friend.

TALE FOUR

The big snake

There was, and there was not, if it hadn't happened it wouldn't have been told, my friend.

Once there was a Gypsy, he had many children, and he was poor. He had a beautiful wife. Well, there's no harm in that. He sets off and leaves his wife in order to find some food for his wife and his children and also to try and get work.

Well then, he went off to the forestlands. He walks and walks until he reached the forest. When he came into the forest who should he meet but a snake.

"Ha! I'm going to eat you, Gypsy!"

"Snake, you will choke! You won't eat me!"

"Oh yes, I'll eat you up!"

"No indeed, you are not going to eat me! But as that is so, we must try our strength and see who's strongest. If you are stronger, then eat me! And if I am stronger, then I'll eat you."

"Yes, good but what shall we try first?"

Let us whistle!"

"Are we going to whistle? Yes, that's very easy," says the snake. "Very well. Which one of us shall whistle first?"

"You whistle first, snake!"

When the snake whistled, the leaves fell off the trees, you understand! Well!

"Eh, that's nothing. That's nothing at all. You did only half as much as I can."

"Oh, are you so strong?"

"Yes indeed! But listen! I feel sorry for you, Snake. If you like... here is my neck-cloth... I'll take it off and blindfold you with it because when I whistle, your eyes will pop out of your head!"

"No, what are you saying Gypsy?"

"Yes, it's true!"

"Alas, I curse your gods but, if that's the way it is, well take your neck-cloth and blindfold me!"

Well, the Gypsy set about covering the snake's eyes with his neck-cloth.

"Now you stay here; I'm going a little further off to get some air!"

He went away and drew a deep breath, and found a stout stick.

"Now I'm going to whistle, Snake! Hold on to yourself and don't be frightened!"

The snake sat down with his back to the tree, and he holds on tight.

"That's right!"

Rap, what a blow he gave him over the eyes! He strikes again. He strikes twice, he strikes three times. Ugh, he fell upon the snake with countless blows. The snake began to cry out:

"Enough, enough, don't anymore! Don't whistle anymore!"

"Indeed!"

"Oh, my eyes were beginning to pop out of my head!"

"So, was it like that! Well, who is the strongest now?"

"You are! Let us become sworn brothers. And just work for each other."

"Good!"

Well, so they went on their way. One day passes, two days pass, three days pass.

"Brother?" says the Gypsy.

"Yes?"

"What would it be like down there near the meadow and down at the edge of the wood. Aren't those oxen going about there and how about if we fetched ourselves an ox and cooked and ate it?"

"Good, yes, you can do that. Off you go, Brother!" said the snake.

He sends the Gypsy off, "Away with you Brother, and fetch us an ox!"

What did the Gypsy do? He just ties the oxen by their tails, he binds them to each other. After a while the snake starts wondering. "What is he doing there, oh God! Maybe people have caught him. I'll go and look for him." So the snake goes down there.

"What are you doing, Brother? I, the snake, am speaking to you. What are you doing?"

"I'm tying them together, Brother, and taking them on my back and bringing them to you."

"Oh, why so much trouble, you should just have taken one, the fattest, which ever it was."

"Yes, but I didn't."

The snake set himself to do it, and he fetches the fattest, the strongest, throws it on his back and goes on his way. When he came back, he took it, the ox, and does so with it – forwards and backwards – and the meat jumps out of the hide. As it came out they just put it in the pot, they cook it, all right.

"Brother", says the snake. "Take the ox hide and go fetch us some water in it! Go!"

Well then, the Gypsy didn't take the ox hide; he set off to the well. He digs a hole on one side, and another on the other side. Once again the snake thinks: Now he is again staying away too long!

"What are you doing here, Brother?"

"I am digging up the well and taking it and carrying it there. Then I won't have to go and fetch water over and over again!"

"Oh, don't do that, Brother!"

The snake just puts the ox hide into the well and fills it with water and puts it on his back and carries it away. Good. Once more the Gypsy did nothing. Well, what is he going to do next? So he walks on a little further. Ready, the water is put on to boil, and the ox put in the pot, but they had no firewood to cook with.

"Brother, go and fetch some firewood for us. Listen, Brother!"

Look what the Gypsy did! He takes linden, that's the kind of tree from which you strip bark, he takes the bark and makes it into ropes and ties up the forest, he binds all around it.

Well, while he is binding it, the snake came back. The snake sees that ...

"What are you doing, Brother?"

"I am tying the forest together, and I put it over my shoulders and I bring it all here at the same time."

"Oh Brother! We aren't going to stay here that long! We're going away, we're leaving soon!"

All right. The snake looks at an old oak-tree and sees that it is dry. He took hold of it and pulls it up from the root, pak! He puts it over his shoulder and walks off. As he arrived there, he thumped it on the ground, and it went to pieces, that tree. Well, the Gypsy sat down and looked sad, he put his hand under his chin, so he did.

Well, the choice soup and the meat are boiling. Now it is ready.

"Come and eat, Brother!"

"No, I don't want to eat!"

"And why not? Are you angry?"

"Not at all!"

"But how is that? Now then, eat!"

"Listen, I don't want to eat!"

"Oh Brother, what have you done, are you angry with me? God be merciful to me!"

"Oh yes, no matter where you sent me, I didn't do as you wanted me to. You sent me to fetch the cattle; I wanted to take them all at one time. You sent me to fetch firewood, I wanted to take the whole forest with me at one time."

"But very well, may God strike him! There wasn't any harm in what you did. You'll do better another time."

"I do everything in a big way when I do it at all."

"All right, Brother, don't let that make you angry. Come and eat!"

"I won't eat!"

"Very well."

Well then, the snake set himself to eat, he does it thoroughly and he scraped the pot with his fingers, because there was far too little. The poor Gypsy didn't venture to eat… Because then the snake would have seen that I eat too little, he thought to himself. And then he would have devoured him. All right! Never mind. He just walks away from there hungry.

Well, as they arrived at the next place still famished:

"Now, what'll we do here, Brother?"

"Well, I don't know what we are to do."

"Then listen now, Brother, what you are to do! Sit here at the edge of the wood. I'm going to the clergyman, I am going."

All right then, he goes off. The snake went to the clergyman. What does he steal: the strong box and two dappled horses and a cart.

Here he comes, driving the cart. Well, as the snake drives along:

"Get in, Brother!"

So the Gypsy got in.

"Now, Brother, now we have horses and a cart and a treasure chest!"

"Yes, very good!"

Early in the morning the snake sees many tents set up on the roadside. The Gypsy's children saw their father and shouted. "There is Daddy, here comes Daddy with the clergyman, here comes Daddy with the clergyman." So they shout, so they hop and skip.

"What are those little ones doing?" asked the snake.

Oh, those are my children."

"So what now?"

"When they saw you they shouted that I am bringing food; and you know Brother, if they see you coming, they'll grab you too, and then they eat you up, and it'll be all up with you."

"But what am I to do?"

"You just hop it!"

The snake turned tail, jumped out of the cart and ran away. And if they are not dead they would still be alive this very day.

TALE FIVE

The cunning boy and the beautiful Gypsy girl

"Well, good day to you, my Gypsy friend."
"Welcome. God has brought you here!" replied the Gypsy.

What is it that the Gypsy's got? A lovely daughter. Many suitors, many Gypsies came to ask for her. But her father and mother say: "Listen! It is not the case that anyone can buy or sell her. That one who can tell the hidden marks that she has on her body, that's the one for whom she is destined."

They guess this, and they guess that. No one can hit upon the marks that she has. Now one day there comes a rich Gypsy. What a beautiful horse he had! Its saddle was made all of silver and gold, and so too its harness. He says:"Good morning, Uncle!"

"Welcome. God has brought you here, my boy!"

"Eh... I've come to ask for your daughter."

"My daughter? I can't give my daughter away. Only the one who can tell the hidden marks she has, that's the one who will have her."

After a little while, with these words he went on his way. That young boy! He was a handsome one. Time passed, a week went by, two weeks, maybe a month. Even a little more than a month passed. The rich Gypsy was forgotten. He dressed himself in shabby clothes, put on torn rags, you could see his skin both in front and behind. He went back to the Gypsy.

"Good morning Uncle!"

"Well, God has brought you here, my boy!"

"I am a poor man, Uncle, motherless, fatherless, and also I have no work."

"Well, my boy! What do you want?"

"I would like to do some work for you."

"What kind of work, I have no work, nothing... except perhaps that you could look after my horses."

For the Gypsy wasn't poor, he owned a house.

Good. He goes to his wife and asks:

"What do you say, wife?"

"Yes, if you like. Let it be so. Take him on! I see it's all right. A good and handsome, reliable fellow, it shows."

So they took him on. He stays for a month, stays for two, even stays for three. He says nothing. But he thinks of nothing but the Gypsy's daughter, of seeing her. And she, where is she? In the mosquito-tent, there she eats and drinks, and sleeps, too.

One day girl's father says: "Listen, my boy! Tomorrow I am going to town with my wife. Only this... I ask of you, that you'll take care of the horses and the girl. Whatever the girl asks for, you are to give her."

"Yes, Uncle, I'll do that"

Good. So off he went.

There was a wretched horse in the stable... and the young Gypsy sets himself to work ... cleans its hooves and just writes on one the horses hooves:

"This horse is not worth two human heads."

Good, so he goes to the merchant.

"Good morning, merchant!"

"God has brought you here, my young man!"

"I have a horse here to exchange with you, sir."

"What kind of horse?"

"Come out and see!"

The merchant looks at the horse's hooves:

"He is worth three human heads,"says the young Gypsy.

"What kind of a horse is that? What kind of horse... well, I have two horses in the stable. Come and look at them!"

The Gypsy tethers his horse to the post and goes into the stable and looks.

"Well, how are we to make an exchange for my two horses?"

"Well, sir. You'll give me the two horses and also some sugar and three or four packets of tea, and you'll also give me two or three biscuits… two or three packets of biscuits."

"I'll do that my boy."

Well, they shook hands on that. When they had shaken hands, they made an exchange… that Gypsy took the horses and left the nag there.

Then he tethered the horses back at the house, put the horses out in the meadow and tethered them much too near each other. Well, one of the two was a colt, as I call it in Romani, h*armigo.*

He tethered them so close to each other that they could touch each other. And when he came, he didn't speak, he said nothing, but put the sugar, the tea and the biscuits aside. And he tethered the horses just opposite the girl's window.

Good, then sleep overcomes him; he laid down his head… and sleeps. The girl calls him.

"The horses are fighting out there. You wretch, you wretch, get up, for the horses are fighting!"

What does he hear, that wretch? He doesn't hear anything! But he saw her naked breast, and her arms are showing. She was in fine shape and a lovely woman.

She shouted again: "You wretch, you wretch, get up for the horses are fighting!"

Well, what shall he do or not do? He gets up… rubs his eyes … for this fellow is pretending. "What do you want, young maiden?"

She got out from under the mosquito net; and then he saw… on her breast, on one side she has a moon, on the other a star. He saw all this. She rushed at him with the whip, lashed him, lashed him so that the blood began to drip from his skin.

So he went to the horses and puts one a little more to the one side, and one a little more to the other and comes home.

"What have you done? You wretch! But if you really had to look at me, you could have come and lifted the mosquito net, and looked at me, and not pretended you were asleep."

"I did sleep. I was tired out."

"You lie!"

"I'm not lying, young maiden!"

Well, listen now, this is what you are to do. Take the samovar and put it on to boil and give me some tea to drink, and you may drink too!"

Well! The boy got up and did so, boiled water in the samovar, put out the tea, put out the biscuits. She questions him, speaks to him.

"Where did you get those horses from?"

"Those... your father had an old nag, and I went to the merchant here and bartered it, and got three hundred roubles, that I got into the bargain, and I got this sugar, and this tea, and these biscuits, I got all that. And those two horses as well."

"Good, you did that well!"

Well then. So the Gypsy couple came home... her mother and her father. The young Gypsy pretended not to know anything. Well, as he doesn't know anything, he gets up and goes: "Thank you, Uncle, I have lived with you for three years. I have eaten and drunk, now I too go and try my luck somewhere further off, Uncle!"

"Now listen, my boy! As you bartered and sold so well, so take these horses for yourself. Or take the three hundred roubles and leave me the horses."

"No, Uncle, I don't need anything."

"Take the three hundred and the horses as well!"

"No? But if you want to give me one of them, all right, or perhaps give me the other horse, so as not to separate the two of them who go well with each other."

The Gypsy gives him another horse and keeps the two horses there. He also gives him fifty roubles for the journey.

One month passed, and two passed, and the young Gypsy cursed "What the hell am I going to do now!"

He began to think. He travelled for one month and for two... nearly half a year. The thought of that girl gnawed at his heart. So then... he finally reaches a decision ... he dressed himself, saddled his horse, put on fine clothes, and off he goes that very night.

"Good morning, Uncle!"

"God has brought you here, my boy!"

The Gypsy doesn't realise now that this was the poor boy from before. Well, what does he want?

" I've come to ask for your daughter, Uncle!"

"My daughter? No, I can't give her up to you. Perhaps if you told me of her secret marks!"

Well, up he gets and he says: "On the right side she has a moon, and on the left a star. Then, what more do you want me to tell you? Aren't those marks enough? Do you want me to tell you about the other mark too?"

You understand what he meant!

"No, no, that is enough! May you be happy!"

So, he gave, that Gypsy did, his daughter to that young boy. And if they are not dead, they are still living today.

Glossary

Kalderash is one of the so-called Vlah dialects of Romani and evolved in Romanian speaking territory from around 1500 when the first Romanies arrived there. There are a large number of loan words from Romanian and we list some below as well as some words of Indian origin which however might not be recognised in the form they occur in the text. On their way from Romania to Sweden the Kalderash passed through many countries and picked up words from Russian not to mention more recently Spanish and French. Readers used to Balkan dialects should note that the translators use 'ts' where more traditional dialects have 'th' (for example tsuv – smoke)

arakhad-	to be born
atsad-	to deceive, trick
atveto	answer
bar	garden
bija	ball
birto	inn
borsalino	*a hat from a factory in Italy*
če,či,čo	your
čid-	to collect
čin-	to buy
čirav-	to boil, cook
čisai	sand
čingo	wet
dakordo	in harmony
dareš	even

dježeš	train
doba	time, moment
dumolo	calm, quiet
fenič	ore
gero	poor
hazna	profit
kasa	(i) cash desk
	(ii) pawnbroker
kher(f.)	boot
kher (m.)	house
koklialo	verdigris
laibero	waistcoat
lavka	shop
matura	motor-car
menča	ball
mubluri	furniture
mužik	landowner
pelerija	hat
perina	eiderdown
pučin-	to pay
pux	feather filling
phenke	he says (=phenel)
raibaro	policeman
rimorko	trailer
skara	ladder, staircase
stena	stage
šantso	hole
šero	head, (here) chapter
šlogo	servant, hired hand
šilav-	to brush
tazo	basin
tsapeno	stiff
tsulo	thick
varo	lime
zadačka	riddle
zaloga	a little bit

The *Interface Collection*

The *Interface Collection* was developed by the Centre for Gypsy Research at the Université René Descartes in Paris in association with publishers throughout Europe and with the support of the European Commission and the Council for Europe. The Centre for Gypsy Research is at the hub of a unique international publishing programme with volumes appearing in up to twelve European languages.

This has been severely curtailed since 2001 by the loss of EU funding for the work of the specialist editorial committees and for the translations organised by the Centre for Gypsy Research and as a result only those volumes which the publishers consider to be commercially viable can now be published. This at present excludes the concluding two volumes in the important series on the Gypsies during the Second World War and further volumes in the series on the Romani language.

For further details about the work of the Centre for Gypsy Research:

Centre de recherches tsiganes
Université René Descartes
45 rue des Saints-Peres
F – 75270 - PARIS Cedex 06,
France

Tel: +33 331 42862112
Fax: +33 1 42862065
E-mail: crt@paris5.sorbonne.fr

We address: http://www.eurrenet.com/

A list of the volumes published so far with the addresses of the publishers follows.

Titles in the *Interface Collection*

Each volume in the *Interface Collection* is published in up to twelve languages (see list of publishers). The English language editions of the *Interface Collection* are published by the University of Hertfordshire Press. Where an English language edition has not been published details of other language editions are given. The code in front of the ISBN identifies the publisher.

An updated version of this list can be seen on the web pages of the University of Hertfordshire Press at: http://www.herts.ac.uk/UHPress/interface.html

1	Marcel Kurtiàde	Śirpustik amare ćhibăqiri (Pupil's book) with Teacher's manual CRDP: ISBN 2-86565-074-X
2	Antonio Gómez Alfaro	The Great Gypsy Round-up PG: ISBN 84-87347-12-6
3	Donald Kenrick	Gypsies: from the Ganges to the Thames UHP: ISBN 1-902806-23-9
4	E. M. Lopes da Costa	On Gypsies: a bibliography of works in Portugese PG: ISBN 84-87347-11-8
5	Marielle Danbakli	Roma, Gypsies: Texts issued by International Institutions UHP: ISBN 1-902806-15-8
6	Bernard Leblon	Gypsies and Flamenco UHP: ISBN 0-900458-59-3
7	David Mayall	English Gypsies and State Policies UHP: ISBN 0-900458-64-X
8	D. Kenrick, G. Puxon	Gypsies under the Swastika UHP: ISBN 0-900458-65-8
9	Giorgio Viaggio	Storia degli Zingari in Italia ANICIA/CSZ: ISBN 88-900078-9-3
10	D. Kenrick, G. Puxon	Bibaxtale Berśa PG: ISBN 84-87347-15-0
11	Jean-Pierre Liégeois	School Provision for Ethnic Minorities: The Gypsy Paradigm UHP: ISBN 0-900458-88-7
12	K. Fings, H. Heuß,	From "Race Science" to the Camps The Gypsies during the Second World War – 1 UHP: ISBN 0-900458-78-X
13	Joint authorship	In the Shadow of the Swastika The Gypsies during the Second World War – 2 UHP: ISBN 0-900458-85-2
14	G. Donzello, B. M. Karpati	Un ragazzo zingaro nella mia classe ANICIA/CSZ: 88-900078-4-2
15	A. Gómez Alfaro E. M. Lopes da Costa Sharon Floate	Deportaciones de Gitanos PG: ISBN 84-87347-18-5 Ciganos e degredos SE: ISBN 972-8339-24-0
16	Ilona Lacková	A false dawn – My life as a Gypsy woman in Slovakia UHP: ISBN 1-902806-00-X
17	Jean-Pierre Liégeois	Ромц, Циганц, Чергарц LIT: ISBN 954-8537-63-X Roma, Sinti, Fahrende PA: ISBN 3-88402-289-X Romák, cigányok, utazók PONT: ISBN 963-9312-43-6

18	Reimar Gilsenbach	Von Tschudemann zu Seemann Zwei Prozesse aus der Geschichte deutscher Sinti	PA: ISBN 3-88402-202-4
19	Jeremy Sandford	Rokkering to the Gorjios	UHP: ISBN 1-902806-04-2
20	Joint authorship	Europe mocks Racism, International Anthology of Anti-Racist Humour (multiple editions)	PG
21	Joint authorship	What is the Romani language?	UHP: ISBN 1-902806-06-9
22	Elena Marushiakova	Gypsies in the Ottoman Empire	UHP: ISBN 1-902806-02-6
23	Joint authorship	La Chiesa cattolica e gli Zingari	ANICIA/CSZ ISBN 88-900078-5-0
24	Joint authorship	Que sorte, Ciganos na nossa escola!	SE: ISBN 972-8339-29-1
25	Ian Hancock, Siobhan Dowd, Rajko Djuric	The Roads of the Roma: a PEN anthology of Gypsy Writers UHP: ISBN 0-900458-90-9 This English language edition was published outside the *Interface Collection*	
26	Santino Spinelli	Baxtaló Divès	ANICIA: ISBN 88-7346-009-7
27	Emmanuel Filhol	La mémoire et l'oubli: l'internement des Tsiganes en France 1940–46	HAM: ISBN 2-7475-1399-8
28	Ian Hancock	We are the Romani People	UHP: ISBN 1-902806-19-0
29	Alyosha Taikon, Gunilla Lundgren	From coppersmith to nurse: Alyosha, the son of a Gypsy chief	UHP: 1-902806-22-0
30	Ján Cangár	L'udia z rodiny Rómov manusa andar e familia Roma	CROCUS: 80-88992-42-7
31	Josef Muscha Müller	Und weinen draf ich auch nicht...	PA: 3-88402-284-9

Série Rukun / The Rukun Series

Eric Hill's popular *Spot the Dog* books in Romani

O Rukun ʒal and-i skòla	Research and Action Group on Romani Linguistics	RB: ISBN 2-9507850-1-8
Kaj si o Rukun amaro?	Research and Action Group on Romani Linguistics	RB: ISBN 2-9507850-2-6
Spot's Big Book of Words in Romani, French and English	Research and Action Group on Romani Linguistics	RB: ISBN 2-9507850-3-4
Spot's Big Book of Words in Romani and Spanish	Research and Action Group on Romani Linguistics	PG: ISBN 84-87347-22-3

Publishers' addresses

ANICIA
Via San Francesco a Ripa, 62
I – 00153 – Roma , Italy
web site:
http://members.it.tripod.de/anicia

CRDP – Centre Régional de
Documentation Pédagogique
Midi-Pyrénées
3 rue Roquelaine
F – 31069 – Toulouse Cedex, France
web site: http://www.crdp-toulouse.fr

CROCUS – Vydavate°stvo CROCUS Nové Zámky
Stefan Safranek
Bernolákovo nám. 27
SK - 940 51 - Nové Zámky
web site:
http://www.crocus.sk

EA – Editura Alternative
Casa Presei, Corp. A, Et. 6
Pia a Presei Libere, 1
RO – 71341 - Bucureşti 1, Bulgaria

EK – Editions Kastaniotis
11, Zalogou
GR – 106 78 – Athèns, Greece
web site: http://www.kastaniotis.com

HAM – Editions L'Harmattan
5-7 rue de l'Ecole Polytechnique
F – 75005 – Paris, France
web site:
http://www.editions-harmattan.fr

IBIS – Ibis Grafika
Sasa Krnic
IV. Ravnice 25
10 000 Zagreb
Croatia
web site:
http://www.ibis-grafika.hr

LIT – Litavra
163 A – Rakovski
BG – 1000 – Sofia, Romania

PA – Edition Parabolis
Schliemannstraße 23
D – 10437 Berlin, Germany
web site: http://www.emz-berlin.de

PG – Editorial Presencia Gitana
Valderrodrigo, 76 y 78
E – 28039 – Madrid, Spain
web site:
http://www.presenciagitana.org

PONT – Pont Kiadó
Pf 215
H – 1300 Budapest 3, Hungary
web site: http://www.pontkiado.com

SE – Entreculturas / Secretariado
Coordenador dos Programas de Educação Multicultural
Trav. das Terras de Sant'Ana, 15 – 1°
PT – 1250 – Lisboa, Portugal
web site:
http//www.min-edu.pt/entreculturas

UHP – University of Hertfordshire Press
Learning and Information Services,
College Lane – Hatfield
UK – Hertfordshire AL10 9AB, Britain
web site:
http://www.herts.ac.uk/UHPress

VUP – Univerzita Palackého v Olomouci – Vydavatelství /
Palacky University Press
Krížkovského 8
CZ – 771 47 – Olomouc, Czech Republic

Distributor for some Rukun titles:
RB – Rromani Baxt
22, rue du Port
F – 63000 Clermont-Ferrand, France

The University of Hertfordshire Press is the only university press committed to developing a major publishing programme on social, cultural and political aspects of the Romani and other Gypsy people who migrated from north west India at the beginning of the last millennium and are now found on every continent. Recent titles include:

We are the Romani People
Ian Hancock (Interface Collection, Volume 28)
ISBN 1-902806-19-0
An introductory guide which presents the most current findings about Romani origins, an overview of politics, culture, language and cuisine, a surprising list of notable people of Romani descent, a description of the centuries-long period of slavery in the Balkans and a brief description of the Romani Holocaust. Especially useful is the chapter on how to interact with Romanies, and the list of recommended readings. Each chapter is accompanied by a list of questions, making it suitable as a textbook for use in class.

Between Past and Future: the Roma of Central and Eastern Europe
Edited by Will Guy
ISBN 1-902806-07-7
This important new study challenges popular misconceptions, analysing how and why Roma have become victims of political and economic restructuring following the overthrow of Communist rule.

A false dawn: my life as a Gypsy woman in Slovakia.
Ilona Lackova (Interface Collection, Volume 16)
ISBN 1-902806-00-X
The inspirational life story of a remarkable woman transcribed and edited from recordings in Romani. The author witnessed the destruction of the Romani culture, language and way of a life in the 'false dawn' of the post war Communist era.

What is the Romani Language?
Peter Bakker et al (Interface Collection, Volume 21)
ISBN 1-902806-06-9
This introductory guide by an international group of specialists in the Romani language describes its origin, current use, the way it is taught and the beginnings of Romani literature and films.

The Roads of the Roma: a PEN Anthology of Gypsy writers
Edited by Ian Hancock, Siobhan Dowd and Rajko Djuric
ISBN 0-900458-90-9
Forty-three poems and prose extracts, most appearing in English for the first time, are arranged alongside an 800-year chronology of repression. What emerges is a portrait of a people struggling to preserve their identity in a hostile world.

Shared Sorrows: a Gypsy family remembers the Holocaust
Toby Sonneman
ISBN 1-902806-10-7
This powerful beautifully written book interweaves the story of the author's own Jewish family with that of the members of an extended family of Sinti survivors of the Holocaust which she came to know in Munich

Gypsies under the Swastika
Donald Kenrick and Grattan Puxon (Interface Collection, Volume 8)
ISBN 0-900458-65-8
The most comprehensive and up to date single volume account of the fate of the Gypsies in the Holocaust.

Gypsies in the Ottoman Empire: a contribution to the history of the Balkans
Elena Marushiakova and Vesselin Popov (Interface Collection, Volume 22)
ISBN 1-902806-02-6
The European part of the Ottoman Empire – the Balkans – has often been called the second motherland of the Gypsies. From this region Gypsies moved westwards taking with them inherited Balkan cultural models and traditions.

Scholarship and the Gypsy struggle: commitment in Romani Studies
Edited by Thomas Acton
ISBN 1-902806-01-8
This book marks the development of a new, authoritative academic approach to Romani Studies which locates itself in the problems identified by the Romani people themselves.

Moving On: the Gypsies and Travellers of Britain
Donald Kenrick and Colin Clark.
ISBN 0-900458-99-2
The only general introduction to the struggle of Gypsies to survive as a people in Britain today.

Smoke in the Lanes
Dominic Reeve
ISBN 1-902806-24-7
A classic account of the reality of life as a Gypsy in the fifties when Travellers lived in horse drawn wagons and stopped by the wayside in quiet country lanes, but were often driven to 'atch' besides main highways as so many of the old stopping-places were fenced-off or built upon. This book is full of stories of life on the road and descriptions of colourful characters living for the present despite constant harassment by police and suspicious landowners

Gaining Ground: law reform for Gypsies and Travellers
Edited by Rachel Morris and Luke Clements (Traveller Law Research Unit, Cardiff Law School)
ISBN 0-900458-98-4
An agenda for reform based on the proposals of professionals and of Gypsies and Travellers themselves.

Roma, Gypsies: Texts issued by International Institutions
Compiled by Marielle Danbakli (Interface Collection Volume 5).
ISBN 1-902806-15-8
A new edition of this essential reference work for libraries, government departments and NGOs of the texts issued on Roma (Gypsies) by all the major international institutions from the European Union to the United Nations.

For further details see:

http://www.herts.ac.uk/UHPress/Gypsies.html

Or request a copy of our catalogue from:

University of Hertfordshire Press
Learning and Information Services
University of Hertfordshire
College Lane
Hatfield
AL10 9AB
Britain

Tel: +44 1707-284654
Fax: +44 1707-284666
E-mail: UHPress@herts.ac.uk